GULLIBLE'S TRAVELS

BILLY CONNOLLY

GULLIBLE'S TRAVELS

*Compiled and introduced
by Duncan Campbell
with illustrations by Steve Bell*

PAVILION
MICHAEL JOSEPH

First published in Great Britain in 1982 by
Pavilion Books Limited
196 Shaftesbury Avenue, London WC2H 8JL
in association with Michael Joseph Limited
44 Bedford Square London WC1B 3DU

Connolly, Billy
    Gullible's travels.
    I. Title
    827'.914   PR6053.0/

    ISBN 0-907516-10-6

Photoset by Rowland Phototypesetting Limited, Bury St Edmunds, Suffolk
Printed by Hollen Street Press Limited, Berkshire
Bound by Robert Hartnoll Limited, Cornwall

CONTENTS

iNTRODUCTiON

The temperature is 109 degrees. An old Indian in a sun hat is quietly raking the gravel on the path. A red, black and green flag is fluttering in the slight breeze. A large lorry is unloading crate after crate of McEwan's Export ale. Another elderly Indian adjusts the direction of the water-sprinkler so that it will just reach the rhododendron bush.

A group of waiters, some Indian, some Bangladeshi, some Pakistani, wearing 'Stop Me and Buy One' T-shirts, are spreading tablecloths over 800 trestle tables in the open air in front of a wide platform, as a loudspeaker blares out a crackly recording of the London Symphony Orchestra at the Proms. A sign says: 'Members are reminded that alcohol-approved cards must be shown prior to purchasing alcohol. Muslims and minors under eighteen are not permitted to consume alcohol on club premises.'

Standing over on the far side of the clubhouse is a large American kitted thus: dark glasses, red and yellow baseball cap, T-shirt, fluorescent green basketball shorts, white socks, running shoes. Over his right shoulder he is carrying a new golf bag bristling with clubs. He gazes out over a golf course that is entirely composed of sand, except for the greens, which are black. In his left hand he is clutching what looks like a sheaf of tickets to something.

Inside the main building, men in safari suits are playing bar billiards on a table made by a firm in St Anne Street, Liverpool.

Another group, cravatted and cologned, are reading the *Daily Telegraph* in the deep brown armchairs, beneath framed prints of old English air balloons, occasionally tapping the ash from a slim cigar into a Dunhill ashtray. They are joined by two young men whose names have just changed places on the badminton ladder. For some reason they are talking to each other in imitations of a Scottish accent. Lagers are ordered all round.

A few miles away in the city which this country club serves, the Chieftain of the Caledonian Society, Bob King, is standing awaiting the guest of honour in the grounds of the British Embassy.

The building could be any British consulate or embassy in any hot country – Karachi or Kuala Lumpur perhaps – with its white paint, Union Jack, cut lawns, whirring fans and self-confidence.

King, a sandy-haired man with one of those honest open faces that Scottish vets have, is wearing brogues, woollen stockings, skean dhu, sporran, kilt and crisp short-sleeved white shirt with a Lothian and Border Police Pipe Band tie.

Along with two other kilted friends, King has been checking that the curry and beer open-air buffet luncheon is ready round the pool; they have a few moments in-between discussing the arrangements to talk about the latest Highland Games in the area and how the tossing the caber had drawn nearly as large a crowd as the camel-racing.

Sitting round the tables by the Hockney pool are a few women, sweating quietly in frocks, fanning themselves occasionally, looking over their shoulders periodically at the tarmac drive with its ramp – for slowing down traffic – and its warning sign which says 'hump' in English and Arabic.

A few moments later a figure with long billowing hair, a beard and an earring – made out of broken glass and shaped like a lopsided heart – bounds along the side of the pool.

The Chieftain shakes his hand and requests a photo of him alongside the three neatly kilted figures. The new arrival poses with them – 'Guess which one didnae graduate!'

Back at the club hours later, the same long-haired figure is greeted by a couple – the man in short-sleeved khaki safari jacket, the woman in a turquoise cocktail dress and gold identity necklace. 'We're frae Falkirk, Billy.'

'Serves you right.'

It's almost dark now and Mercedes and Rovers are gliding into place outside the club. The microphone is tested by an amiable Scot while a waiter asks why it is that people testing microphones *always* say: 'Testing-one-two-three, testing'. No one knows why. The tables are now piled high with McEwans and Heinekens and white wines nestling in fibreglass iceboxes. Flying beetles zip in and out of the spotlight. A banjo, guitar and autoharp are put on stage by a roadie who places each object in its position as reverently as an altar boy. The fairy lights round the edges of the enclosure dim. The main spotlight comes on.

'Helllloooo, Dubai,' says the man as he comes on stage to delighted applause. And within minutes a strange collection of expatriate quantity surveyors, oilmen, Embassy officials, British Caledonian cabin crews, engineers from Ruislip, contractors from Kilmarnock, export dealers from Carlisle, are listening transfixed.

'Did you catch the royal engagement?' he asks, since it is the summer of eighty-one. 'Did you notice how they announced it on the day of the latest unemployment figures . . . I wonder what they'll do for the next lot – find a man for the Queen Mother, I suppose.'

'Shame, shame,' comes from some of the more patriotic enclaves of the audience.

'Aw, c'mawn . . . I'm one of these people who likes Britain so much he *lives* there. Relax and enjoy yourselves: you're out here making a fortune while there's millions on the dole. There's people who would *love* to be here . . . Mind you, there's some who'd laugh at you as soon as they leave.'

Members of the audience, feeling the effects of the beers, who have to go to the gents' and ladies' on the far side of the wicker fence, are greeted with: 'Christ, what's this? A bloody sponsored walk or something?' And those who shout back get: 'If my dog had a face like yours I'd shave its arse and make it walk backwards!' in return.

Two hours later, the show over and the strains of 'Tell Laura I Love Her' dying away, a group of young Scots build a pyramid of McEwan's cans on one of the tables and when the club president Iain Valentine asks them to desist he gets a biff in the eye and has to get first aid in the clubhouse. Elsewhere the waiters swap one-liners with the Evening's Attraction as he loads his guitar.

A homesick young man from Dundee stumbles down the pathway to the car park, repeating one of the evening's jokes. He stops. And kneeling down gently beside a patch of hydrangeas, watered only that afternoon, he is quietly sick all over them.

It is the eve of the Cup Final. Tottenham Hotspur versus Manchester City. Traditionally there is an eve-of-final dinner for the footballing aristocracy. This year it is in the Nine Kings suite of the Royal Lancaster hotel and doubles as the *Sunday People*'s Soccer Merit Awards Ceremony.

Since there are prize-giving, speeches and sport, the whole evening has the aura of end of term at a very athletic boys' school. Almost the only women to be seen are waitresses.

The host is Jimmy Tarbuck. The audience consists of dozens of sportsmen past and present, footballers and cricketers, rugby stars and golfers, boxers and judo experts and jockeys and sprinters and swimmers, with contingents of journalists and managers and agents, almost all discussing sport over the melon with prawns. There is much drinking.

As a preview to the prize-giving, there is a spotlighting – literally – of the great and near-great in the audience. So famous names of what is referred to as 'yesteryear' are called up by name and hover over the prawns for a round of applause.

Each new recipient of a mention is given a generous hand, although the enthusiasm wanes slightly by the time the *ananas viole orientale* have arrived and some of the older stars are murmuring 'Who?' as young Turks in double-breasted suits take a bow. (And when the MC calls out for 'one of our great tennis-players' to stand up, a retired cricketer suggests: 'They'll be inviting up one of the great English astronauts next'.)

Mr Tarbuck knows his audience well and there is a remark for every recognisable face: 'Lawrie McMenemy – a legend in his own mind . . . Kenny Lynch was telling me – through his interpreter . . .'

One table is full of World Cup heroes: Bobby Moore, Nobby Stiles, Gordon Banks and six of the others in the team. There is much swapping of autographs. But by the stage of the evening when the final introductions are being made, some of the intended honourees have slipped out for a pee and the spotlight desperately circles the room, lighting up the occasional laden-down Greek waiter.

As the brandy glasses are filled and the air gets smokier, the night becomes rowdier. One of the few women to win an award stands up in the spotlight and is rewarded with remarks about her body from a tableful of cricketers. And as a harassed, elderly Italian waitress attempts to clear the table, a Distinguished Former Test Cricketer curses her: 'Fucking foreigners – coming over here and taking our jobs.' The rest of the table stiffens slightly. The DFTC regards a sportswoman at the far table: 'Christ, she's built, isn't she? I bet she bangs like a shithouse door!'

The speeches flow on: 'This goalkeeper was known as The Cat – he kept giving his defence kittens . . . I'd like to pause a moment for absent friends: the wine waiter . . . But, seriously, it's wonderful how they managed to get the soup the same temperature as the wine . . . There's three babies in a Belfast maternity ward: one German, one Jewish, one Irish – how do they tell which is which? One salutes, the other shits himself and the third wipes it on the wall . . . When they introduced metrication in Ireland they had to put the school leaving age up to thirty-eight . . . Nice to see Malcolm's wife here – she's been to the hairdressers I see. It was closed . . . I haven't seen so much cheap jewellery since Liberace walked down the stairs at the

London Palladium . . . I've been drunk for three days: yesterday, today and tomorrow.' The DFTC laughs loudly though he lets the rest of his table know that he can be a lot funnier himself.

Finally it is time for the Guest of Honour – 'Someone get a blanket,' says Tarbuck by way of introduction, 'Billy's been sick.'

The guest of honour starts off with a few words about masturbation: 'I find I have to do it twice in the morning just to get my heart started.'

'Christ,' says the DFTC disapprovingly, 'that's a bit *bloody strong*, isn't it?' And as the other thoughts on masturbation, Jesus and Ian Paisley come tumbling out from the top table, the Distinguished Former Test Cricketer makes his excuses and leaves, disgusted.

A July evening in Grapevine, Texas. A party of about forty on the annual staff outing for a local bank are sauntering down to 308 Main Street, the home of the Grapevine Oprey.

Across the road, at the Rib Tickler Café – 'our meals are in a sack' – a counter-hand is dispensing spare ribs, smoked sausage, brisket, beans and root beer. The diners sit under the trees, licking the barbecue sauce off their fingers.

The bank staff are due to be entertained by Melissa Ann, a ten-year-old who will sing 'Coat of Many Colours', and a Japanese country-and-eastern band called The Lost City Mad Dogs. Coming attractions include 'Direct from Nashville, Tammy Whitehead', 'Bob Miller (Sings like Ray Price)' and 'Handsome Craig Dillingham'. Melissa Ann, with half an hour to curtain up, is serving popcorn at the ticket office, her hair still in curlers.

With time to kill the bank staff move out into the open to drink a Lone Star beer and chat about the show, the air controllers' strike and . . . that strange sight that greets them in the parking lot opposite.

A weirdo in a cowboy shirt is busy throwing a folding frisbee – a new craze in Dallas it seems – into the air, shouting and leaping as it is thrown back. 'Careful,' he shouts, 'that's the Pope's bloody hat you've got there!' It's really too hot for that sort of stuff and fully-grown men in their thirties don't usually play frisbee and shout profanities in the main street of Grapevine. Must be *on* somethin'.

All of which proves three things: that expatriate quantity surveyors, former Test cricketers and Texan bank clerks find different things funny; that it can get damned hot abroad; and that Billy Connolly manages to get about a bit.

Which is by way of introduction to this guide to the world, travel, life, death and camel-smells as seen through the eyes of, well . . .

'a breath of foetid air, the gangling Glaswegian doyen of bad taste' (John Coldstream, *Daily Telegraph*) . . . 'the Caliph of Crudity, the Emperor of Embarrassment' (*What's On*) . . . 'the man who makes Bette Midler look like Jess Conrad' (Moira Petty, *The Stage*) . . . 'one of the most outrageous Scotsmen ever to have vaulted Hadrian's Wall' (*Daily Express*) . . . 'an explosion in a horsehair sofa' (*Melody Maker*) . . . 'the laughing laureate of the loo, the bawdy bard of bodily behaviour' (Robert Shelton, *The Times – The Times*) . . . 'Marcel Marceau couldn't do better' (Dave Gelly, *The Observer*) . . . 'I was told to "fuck off, you wee bastard" and kicked up the backside with his pointed toe boot' (Hugh Farmer, *Sunday People*, giving evidence at Stirling Sheriff's Court) . . . 'his choice of clothes does nothing for the image of fashion in Scotland' (Raj Shah, jeans manufacturer, announcing his Worst-dressed Men list) . . . 'King of the wisecrack, Duke of the tantalisingly constructed joke' (*Belfast Newsletter*) . . . 'A King Charles in jeans' (*Daily Telegraph*) . . . 'Is it necessary for him to have that silly goatee beard and keep sweeping the hair off his face like a big lassie? Doesn't he know that short back and sides is back in fashion now?' (Reader's letter in the *Daily Mail*) . . . 'an example of the true Scottish identity' (*The Tablet*) . . . 'unique and universal' (*Financial Times*).

And the welder who got away with it.

Duncan Campbell

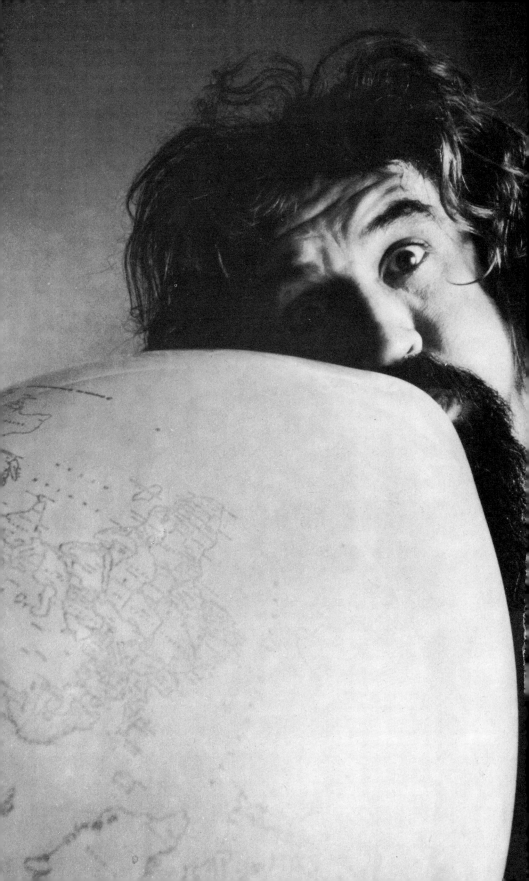

People say it's easy on the road. That it's all swimming pools and sunshine and glamour. And they're right.

But in the early days it was all sleeping rough – I've slept on so many floors I can tell the difference between Axminster and Wilton by the taste. And in those days it was about seven pounds you got for a gig. Now I throw more money at a dog if I haven't got a stone.

Some roadies are only happy when they're travelling. They're real road rats. I've had that thing myself a wee bit, like that lovely Incredible String Band song: 'I've been chained to the land since the day I was planned and my feet surely ache for the road'. I know what they mean. Teddy Prendergast's roadie is on the road with him about three hundred nights a year and when he gets a few days off he goes off with the Stones or something. But at the moment I'm spending so much time on the road that I'm on first-name terms with the traffic wardens. And with all the luggage we cart around I feel like Zsa Zsa Gabor.

Most roadies take terrible care of themselves: they live off codeine sandwiches for breakfast and meat pies and vodka. No wonder they've all got as much fat on them as a bicycle, as much muscle as a butcher's pencil.

One evil trick that roadies have is to put a vibrator in your suitcase so that when you're going through customs, everyone sees it and you're going: 'How the hell did that get in there?' and everyone else around you is going: 'Oh-ho!'

I've never quite worked vibrators out. I think reps buy them. Drive home in the Cortina with the suit hanging in the back and give the wife a surprise . . . 'What are you doing, dear? Is that a torch? Going to put the cat out are you?' I'd like to meet the first vibrator baby.

Another thing roadies like to slip into the luggage is Durex. I never understood how you were meant to put Durex on. I mean, you can't arrive with it on, can you? 'Oh, hi . . . that? Oh, I just put it on in the bath to save drying my willie.' So at what stage in the proceedings are you meant to put it on? Right in the middle of all the activity?

'Oh, excuse me – I'll keep the bed shaking by rocking it with my foot while I put this on . . .' I'm not sure.

One thing you encounter in the continental hotels is the bidet. I washed my feet in the first one I came across. I thought . . . Hmm, that's very handy. Nice of them to put one of those in. But one of the disadvantages of travelling with loonies to football games in Europe is that they always, always shit in the bidet.

Hotels can be the grimmest places on earth. Especially if there's a couple making love in the next room like they've just heard the four-minute warning and you feel very sorry for yourself because all you want to do is curl up with someone like two spoons in a drawer.

I'd love to sleep in silk sheets but for some reason they have always eluded me. I've slept in nylon ones but you always end up getting your toenail caught in them which isn't very romantic.

A great hotel game to play when you're on tour and really, really bored is Room Service Fancy Dress: you all meet in the lobby or foyer or whatever the hell you want to call it and agree a time – one-thirty a.m. That's the deadline. Then you all have to rush off and be back in the lobby by that time having dressed up in fancy dress. The rule is that you can only use things in your room – lampshades, sheets, those candlewick bedspreads, towels etc. Then you have to get back to the lobby and stand stock-still. The real fun is seeing everyone else looking at these loonies standing in a bunch of sheets, with lampshades and sunglasses on.

One odd thing I've noticed about hotels in Britain is that whenever you ask for the *Morning Star* you never get it. They will get you anything else – the *Shropshire Star* or what have you – but for some reason they won't get you the *Morning Star*. You can ask for the *John o' Groats Journal* and they'll say: 'I'll try my very best,' but you ask for the *Morning Star* and you can get a funny look from the night porters, one of those 'Uh-huh, not sure about this one here' looks.

The wee hotels are usually the nicest. They're not full of people looking down their noses at you because they still regard entertainers as sort of gypsies. I love all those little towns in England where they don't get too many people coming through. The concerts are always great – someone's made the cakes and put them in the dressing room and there's always tea in those big fat brown English teapots. It's not like the big halls where it's a bit like clocking-on at the factory . . . 'Hello, Bill, your room's the same as last time.'

What I can't stand in hotels are those lamps that you find everywhere – the ones that look like big globules of glue, as though someone's been interfering with themselves in the bath.

Lots of hotels are so alike you wouldn't know whether you were in Australia or Wyoming. But I heard that Stevie Wonder likes Holiday Inns because everything is always in the same place so I suppose there's that to be said for them.

T-shirts are one of the things you keep picking up as you travel along. I have some favourites – one that was around during the big Born-Again time in America. It had 'Jesus Loves You' on the front, 'And he fucking hates you' on the back . . . We wanted to have tour jackets – those flashy, satin numbers – with 'Pope John Paul World Tour 1981 Road Crew' on the back but it was thought that this would be in bad taste.

Frankie Miller had a nice T-shirt that said 'Frankie who?' on the front. And on the back: 'Frankie Fucking Miller.'

I've got a great T-shirt which just says: 'Fuck 'em if they can't take a joke' on it.

Another lovely T-shirt I saw was at this sci-fi convention that was taking place in Boston at the hotel where we were staying. I saw one of the delegates in a lift and he was wearing all sensible clothes – tweed jacket, ordinary trousers, sensible shoes, glasses – and he had on this T-shirt which said: 'No, but I look like him'. All the people at the convention were great – there was one bunch who were all *green* and wearing silver capes. They really got into it. The same thing in England and you'd just have guys in blazers and Hush-puppies.

At night the sci-fi people would have a party and they were all folkies. It wasn't David Bowie and Ground Control, it was all folk songs, the funny ones that get called novelty items on the Hit Parade

— things like the one about people trapped on a Boston subway —
'And he never returned' — and one of the blokes' wives puts his
sandwiches through the window. They would sit cross-legged on
the floor and sway from side to side, like a Cairngorm ski night. The
only remotely sci-fi songs they would do would be things like 'Flying
past Uranus' and rubbish like that. I think they were the kind of
people who'd originally got into folk because it was a bit weird and
then got into sci-fi because it was nice and weird, too.

The sci-fi convention itself was funny. Authors you'd never heard of
sitting round signing funny-shaped books. The hucksters do big
business with sci-fi mags from the forties — the *Eagle* was even on
sale for the Dan Dares and Mekons. And *Star Trek* was big; they
didn't like those intergalactical hows-your-father modern ones,
they liked Spock. He came from Boston and was a local hero. I was
buying lots of T-shirts and caps for my children and the sci-fi people
said: 'Where are you from?' 'Scotland.' They thought I'd come all
the way for the convention and so I was treated like a lord and of
course I wasn't letting the cat out of the bag. (When did people keep
bloody cats in bags anyway?)

They had these sci-fi jackets as well, the cutaway ones . . . which
reminded me of the old one in Scotland about: 'Can I have a maroon
jacket for ma roon' shoulders, please.'

Americans even have messages on their belt buckles. We found one
which said :'Syphilis — Scourge of the American Youth', which I
suppose you're meant to notice as you take your trousers off. Or to
attach to a Bible belt.

Travelling underwear should always be cotton — never nylon or you
get this awful irritation which they call Jock Itch in America. Sounds
like a football commentator. They treat it with something called
Lui, some strange thing that magically turns to powder, a sort of
white vapour.

Hotel soaps make you itchy as well. I suppose the soaps themselves
are fine until they're mixed with all the foreign water. They're
probably tested in London or New York where the water's different. Anyway, the local waters make the soap stick to your body in
white streaks, like cheap shoes in the rain.

I wanted to take a camouflage jacket with me on my last tour but we went into the warehouse where they keep them at the Army and Navy stores and we couldn't find them anywhere.

Boiler suits have always fascinated me. Those terrible ones with the eleven-inch turn-ups and the crutch away down below the knee . . . 'Aye, the wife bought them.' From the back it looks like your bum just fainted.

One clothing thing that has always puzzled me: why do rugby-players' shorts have pockets and fly-buttons on them? Rugby players puzzle me, too. I can't understand why they stop them playing because they've got brain damage – I would have thought it was a positive advantage. They have these amazing hi-jinks after games – spoof rugger games in the hotel corridors, bread roll fights. If any of our lot did the same thing – when we were away on weekends in Arran in our schooldays – it was regarded as danger-ous. Because we weren't laughing while we were doing it.

When I'm on the road I always have to have a good pen. You need a decent one for signing autographs – if you've just got a Bic, they think you're on the skids.

I had an odd experience in Fraser's in Glasgow just before Christ-mas. I was in buying presents as is my wont, and the woman behind the counter recognised me and asked for my autograph. 'Sure. There you go.' Then two minutes later I'm writing out a cheque to pay for the gear and I didn't have a banker's card or anything, just the cheque. And she wouldn't accept it because I didn't have any identification.

Always beware of strange lavvie paper. I was at a party at Hamish Imlach's once and there was lavvie paper there which he'd been using for painting and it was all covered in paraffin. So I wiped my arse with it. Agony. I had to get into the bath to try and cool it down. Same thing happened in Doha – the people we were staying with took us out on their yacht – oh, yes, it's not all glamour, you know – and the owner of the yacht got oil on his trunks and was trying to wipe it off with turps. Suddenly he just leaped off the boat into the water, the pain was so bad.

Toothbrushes for travel should always be the simplest you can find. Don't get one of those fancy-angled ones with a bit of floss at the end because you will miss it terribly when you lose it, as I guarantee you will. Dental floss is addictive, which is worth bearing in mind.

I've never understood people who travel with wigs – as they used to say in Glasgow: 'Why pay good money for a wig when you can get the same effect by putting glue on your head and sticking it into a barber's midden.'

One thing you see people carting around with them everywhere nowadays is a pocket calculator. What's everybody calculating all of a sudden? And some of them play wee tunes, like 'Jingle Bells'. Do blokes think this makes them attractive to women? Though I liked a wee cartoon I saw in the paper: some run-down shabby office and the boss is saying to his secretary: 'Send them a bill for fifteen million and they'll think we've got a computer.'

You get people with those travelling games as well – backgammon. Until I was a showbiz personality I thought that was something you ate.

And those wee Mickey Mouse watches. It's great. When you get bored you can try and get Mickey's balls into his ears.

Books are essential if you're on the move at all. Most of the time you'll be travelling when you're reading and being shoogled around quite a bit so I don't take anything that requires too much concentration.

At the beginning of my tour in the Middle East, I was reading Stuart Christie's autobiography which was good as he tells you about all the cock-ups and doesn't try and make himself a hero – because the thing with Franco was a bit of a flop at the end. But I had to stop reading it because it was beginning to dominate the way I felt about everything around me – like reading Orwell. Aye, Stuart was very windswept and interesting but he's made it hard for the rest of us to get through Customs without being searched!

Another one I read on the road was Gordon Liddy's *Will*. What a shocker. He used to burn himself to show what an amazing will he had – all the sizzling flesh and smell to do that. The last chapter of the book is about his kids and the last line is 'Tomorrow belongs to Them', which shows you where he's at. He chose his wife because of her Aryan looks as being a better strain for his children than the dark-haired woman he'd been going out with. He sang the Horst Wessel song to impress the black guys in prison and he showed reruns of Nuremburg in the White House. It's frightening to think that someone like that can get so high up. Not that there's much difference between Nixon and Reagan. And Liddy, when he's doing his time in jail, finds out that there's a reporter who's got into the jail as a prisoner to try and interview him. So he passes the word around. The guy ends up getting brutally raped – 'they tore his ass' it says in the book. A really creepy guy.

And I read Shere Hite's report on male sexuality. But the trouble with a book like that, that asks people to talk about their sexual fantasies, is that people always fantasise about their fantasies so you don't ever know if you're getting the real ones. Everyone was surprised that she found that American men like masturbating a lot. It doesn't surprise me.

One big disadvantage of travelling is that you lose touch with what's happening. You can't get newspapers so you end up with those news magazines like *Time* and *Newsweek* and all you get is a very biased view of the world. Like when the riots were going on in England I wanted to be there so I could find out what was really happening but we were in Australia or Hong Kong or somewhere. But I did discover in Doha the first person in the world I've ever met who was sorry that *Now!* magazine wasn't coming out any more.

I've never liked the porn mags. Even *Playboy* I feel is terribly cheap and nasty. I don't like being manipulated by a magazine because I do find them titillating like everyone else and I'm not sure I like being titillated and having my emotions and hormones messed around with, especially by Hugh Hefner.

But I've often looked in the windows of those sex shops and wondered what to do with all the things they sell. I mean, those bits of string with two balls with a wee loop on them. What do you actually do with that?

And those rubbers you see in Amsterdam that look like rough pickles, all warts and everything. I saw one there which, instead of the wee bag they have at the front to catch the precious bodily fluids in, had Fred Flintstone with his arms and legs stretched out. Poor Freddy. I always imagined him going in and shouting 'WILLLL-MAAAA . . .' as he disappeared.

I think about ninety per cent of the trade done in those shops is through people buying stuff to embarrass other people. Those big thick rubbers, the ones that last for ever, they're amazing. I'm surprised Sir Robert Mark doesn't advertise them: 'I believe these are a genuine contribution to safety.' It's funny you can drive round the Grand Prix circuit advertising cigarettes and booze and no one says a thing but when they tried to advertise Durex, everyone panicked. They didn't want the kiddies to see it.

Which is daft. Because at school you get taught nothing about it all. I was married eleven years before I found out what a douche was. I'd always had a vague idea and in fact it turned out to be right but I didn't know for sure.

And Tampax. When we first came across that in a midden we read the instructions on the packet and thought 'Naw . . . ye cannae dae that to yourself.' And when we saw them we thought they were bandages for a really bad cut. It was like a giant Elastoplast. It seemed like the oddest thing I had ever seen in my life. Because no one would ever dream of explaining it to us beforehand.

The woman who lived downstairs from us when I was a kid had a broken pipe and she wrapped round it what I thought was a wee hammock – it turned out to be a sanitary towel – and one of the neighbours, Gerry, went down to fix it and I remember him saying: 'Aw, for fuck's sake – that's disgusting!' and I thought: What can be disgusting about that? Then later on I would see them in middens and get to wondering what they could possibly be.

The American sex shops must be the most bizarre. They sell these inflatable dolls and also sell just the head – supposedly for people to drive along the freeway with.

I've only been to one strip club in my life. It was down in Blackpool during the Glasgow Fair weekend and it was that time when they had to stand completely still – after the law changed you'd hear the guys in Soho shouting: 'Naked And She Moves'. So Stella was her name and all the Glasgow guys were trying to make her giggle so she'd move. The weirdest thing was that there was a man there, a terrible emaciated bloke in a bikini lying on a bed, supposedly as a warning as to what happened to women who indulged in loose living and got VD. But it was a bloke! And the announcer would say: 'This used to be a very beautiful woman,' and point at him. And the strippers would come on as all these different historical characters: Mary Queen of Scots, Dick Turpin, someone from the Roman Empire. They changed their hats and that was all – no clothes on but a different hat for each part.

Round where I was living in Fulham you'd see all those sex ads in shops. 'Miss Busty', 'Miss Sadista' and so on. 'It's a great life if you don't weaken,' which I suppose is some code for discipline. I suppose all those spanking places are aimed at ex-public schoolboys who got beaten a lot and that would be the only physical contact they had with anyone during their formative years. Something like that, anyway.

Enemas are also popular with that crowd, too. Possibly it has associations with matron – I don't know. And another thing is to be locked in a cupboard without your dinner. Why not?

One place I noticed in Soho was advertising all these exotic sexual aids – things you put your willie in and a sort of suction thing is wrapped round which is apparently a big hit. But the entrance to this place is tucked away, very discreet, and it's right next door to this café. And it looks as though lots of punters look in the window, very surreptitious, then dash into what they think is the shop – they find themselves in their dirty mac in the middle of this wee café asking for a French tickler. They probably get served a salami sandwich with a feather in it.

1

1. Aye, they really do exist.

2. You should taste the soup in this place.

3. Who says that Australia doesn't produce intellectuals? A typical Sydney graffiti.

2

3

HYGIENE
AND FITNESS ON THE ROAD

wo of the great problems of travelling are loneliness and poor health. I'm fortunate in that I've found a way of combating both at once: masturbating. When you're in a country with no leeches, have a good wank.

People think that there's only one way of doing it. But I've discovered a great new way. You lie on your arm until it's gone dead. *Then* you do it. And it feels like somebody else.

That piece of advice has helped unfortunate welders and engineers to get through their contracts in the desert. One does what one can.

But there's no doubt that it is the devil's work. You go blind if you do it. Though I know people who've done it just until they were short-sighted and then stopped. I've always reckoned I'd just do it until I needed glasses.

The real experts are to be found on the oil rigs. They rock more at night than during a storm. The blankets fall off the beds there – and break.

Still, some doctors take it all too seriously. Like cutting people's right arms off because they think they're going blind.

The main three illnesses you have to watch out for in world-travelling are cancer, heart attacks and Jeep Bottom.

Jeep Bottom is a disease that members of the working class don't get. It comes from having your arse bang up and down in a Range Rover. You have to carry a wee cushion around with you wherever you go. I've had a variation of it: Jag Jacksie, which was most painful. Also Cherokee Cheeks should be watched out for. The problem is that not enough people know about the disease. Myself, for many years I thought Jeep Bottom was a wee village in Dorset.

Cancer. The greatest diet known to man. For some reason you're not meant to make jokes about it . . . 'Oh, poor old Auntie Judy died o' cancer, ye shouldnae joke about it, son . . .' But everyone dies of something. No one ever died of death. The fatality rate of breathing is a hundred per cent. But for some reason cancer has got this big thing attached to it. It's a lot of hypocrisy . . . you get the relatives going in to visit the bloke in the cancer ward and then going: 'Where have you hid the Embassy coupons, you old bastard?'

Heart attacks should be avoided if possible. The hotel we stayed at in Dallas had a little heart-attack machine where you shove your finger in a hole – this is true – and you get a reading as to how healthy you are. I came out in the second healthiest category which pleased me greatly. Then my roadie did it and came out as of Olympic fitness so I don't believe in them any more.

One place not to have any kind of illness is America. You go to an American doctor with dandruff and you end up with open-heart surgery through the foot. The doctors have cash registers instead of stethoscopes. You come in and tell them you've got cancer and they go: 'Happy days are here again!'

The Queen was visiting a military hospital in Scotland. The big sergeant major was showing her round. She came to the first bed. A soldier lying face down. Groaning. 'Ohhhhh . . . ahhhhh . . . ohhhh, Ah'm no' well. Ah'm no' a well person. I'm decidedly unhappy . . .'
    'What's wrong with this fellow here?'
    'Haemorrhoids, ma'am.'
    'Oh, it must be awful sore. What sort of treatment does he receive?'
    'Wire brush and Dettol, ma'am.'
    'The poor man's arse must glow in the dark. Do you mind if I talk to him?'
    'Go right ahead, ma'am. It's your hospital.'
    'Well, soldier, can I ask you: do you have any ambitions left?'
    'Oh, yes, ma'am. As soon as Ah'm better, Ah want tae get out o' here and get back tae daein' ma duty for you and the country.'
    'That's wonderful. This man should have a medal for that.' So she gets a medal, pins it to the back of his pyjamas and moves on to the next bed. There's a man lying there face up, looking rather green round the gills.
    'What's up with this chap?'
    'Venereal disease, ma'am. Self-inflicted injury. No sympathy for him at all.'
    'Oh, I've read about that. It sounds terrible. What treatment does he receive?'

'Wire brush and Dettol, ma'am.'

'Oh, the poor man's willie must be in tatters.' She goes over to the bed. 'Hello, soldier.'

'Hello yourself, ma'am. Nice tae see you.'

'Have you any ambition left in life?'

'Oh, yes, tae get rid of this disgusting disorder so that Ah can get back and start daein' ma duty again for you and the country.'

'Very good . . . Give me another medal . . . No, a bigger one . . . There you go.' And she pins the medal on his pyjamas. She goes up the ward and there's a third guy – there's always three guys in these stories – sitting up in bed. Doesn't look too sick.

'What's wrong with you, soldier?'

'Laryngitis, ma'am,' he says in this low whisper.

'Oh, I've had that before with all the speaking engagements I've had. It's no joke, is it? What kind of treatment are they giving you?'

'Wire brush and Dettol, ma'am.'

'Good God – and have you any ambitions left in life?'

'Yes, ma'am – to get the wire brush and Dettol before those filthy bastards down there!'

One treatment that has always fascinated me is the enema. I wonder who invented it. Can you imagine someone thinking: 'Hmm, this seems like a good idea – shove something up your jacksie and whoosh.' But even more interesting – who would be the first patient to allow someone to do that?

I'm not that impressed with the state of health of a lot of my audiences. You ask them to clear their throats before they join in a chorus and the hall sounds like a TB ward. They say they've got a 'frog in their throat'. That's rubbish. The only way you'd get a frog in your throat is if you sleep at the bottom of a pond. It's only called a frog because it's green. It's just a wee snotter, that's all.

Crabs is an ailment they should find a new name for. I got some crabs from a wee local fish bloke in Olympia and took them home. 'Hey – I've got crabs, dear.' Didn't go down too well.

I have the occasional wee refreshment on the road. I love that expression – 'a wee refreshment'. You hear it all the time in the Sheriff's Court in Glasgow. Guys done for drunk and disorderly. 'Ah'm very sorry, your honour, Ah'd had a wee refreshment.'

People have this idea that I must be pissed when I go on stage, which I never am. Afterwards, it's different. Though I did see myself on the video and looked really drunk and hungover and puffy so I cut down. If I gave up drinking completely for the sake of my health, I'd be bound to be killed in a plane crash.

But sometimes when I've got a terrible hangover and my head feels like a telephone exchange and my mouth's like a hedgehog's crutch, I swear I'll never touch another drop. That's one disadvantage about becoming a vegetarian – you get drunk a lot quicker.

The only trouble with not drinking is waking up with a headache and having nothing to blame. But not drinking – and a bit of meditating – make an awful difference to how you perform; because in this game you can drink a lot and get away with it and people say: 'Och, he's a loonie,' and let you get on with it.

The one drink to avoid is Advocat: the alcoholic's omelette. That gives you a terrible hangover, too: your mouth feels like it's had a tongue transplant and the new one doesn't fit.

Most of the food you get on the road is rubbish: things out of the Battered Saveloy Refuge. Though I have to confess to suffering from an occasional Mac Attack. This is a desperate desire to eat a McDonald's hamburger which must be resisted at all costs.

I miss not being able to make my own food – particularly now that I make such delightful pastry. I can even make those wee pastry flowers on the top of pies. You probably know the song – 'Oh, Flower of Pastry, When will we see your like again'.

We used to have our own fresh eggs in Scotland. We bought a dozen chickens from one of those horrible factory places and everyone said they'd never survive in normal conditions. But we took them home, put them in a wee hut for forty-eight hours so that they'd know it was home, and then let them out. They'd only ever been on a concrete floor before so they had no idea what life was about.

When they first came out it was snowing. They didn't know what the hell was going on and all stayed in a wee huddle, none of them wanting to be the one on the outside, making that gwwwaaawwwkkk noise. You would keep finding them stuck down a rabbit burrow with their wee bums in the air, because they didn't know what was what.

And I saw a show on telly that said that the battery chicken was specially bred and they'd never know how to be a real chicken. Total and absolute bullshit. Because these chickens in two weeks were doing chicken things, pulling up worms and everything – although George the cockerel wasn't a battery one so he may have taught them – they might have had night classes in the coop with George.

If I'd known I was going to live this long, I'd have taken better care of myself. Did I overindulge myself in my youth? Are the Kennedys gun-shy? But you know that awful feeling in the bath when you notice that one of your pubic hairs is grey. They don't start receding, do they? End up looking like a Kentucky Fried Chicken . . .

I don't want to cut my hair in case there's a geriatric underneath. Perhaps if I took it off I'd be grabbed for being Lord Lucan. It's weird when some of your contemporaries start to look like old men – red faces and pot bellies. Ah, well. It comes to us all.

I dyed my hair ages ago. Lilac. It was quite a brave thing to do in Glasgow. But the dye kept running so it was changing colour every week. Every week a new adventure. Then it ended up as a sort of Hooker Blonde.

They used to have barbers in Glasgow with a sign in the middle of the window that said: 'Haircuts repaired'. I know what they meant. Those awful cheap haircuts you'd get and someone would say: 'Aye, that haircut'll no' last ye the week.'

Pimples are a bit of a problem when you're travelling. At least they're acceptable. When I did that album, *The Pick of Billy Connolly*, the advertising people were writing a promo for it to advertise it on the telly and they ran into awful problems with that body – what's it called? the IBA? or the STD? or the PIA – Pain In the Arse. They sent the ad back with red lines through just about everything and the only word they allowed was 'pimple'.

Itchy bums are another hazard. That's that terrible affliction when your bum gets itchy in a busy street. It's amazing. Your bum *never* gets itchy at home. It's always in the middle of a pedestrian precinct. And if you're in a pair of tight jeans – you can't get near it. It accounts for some weird walks – when you're trying to get the two halves of your arse to rub against each other. The solution to this is very simple: all you do is stand with your legs apart and say in a loud voice: 'My God, my arse is incredibly itchy – I think I'm going to give it a good scratch.' And everyone will look away so you can get on with it in peace.

The great thing about being a showbiz personality is that you don't fart any more. You get a fartectomy in Harley Street. When I got mine done, Princess Anne was in the queue behind me. I don't think hers worked: she still looks like a horse just shit in her handbag.

Trying to get out of bed after someone just farted is like trying to get out of a quicksand. I don't believe the Queen farts. If she does, it's blue.

It's important, of course, to check on your jobbies to make sure you're still in good health . . .
    A Glasgow councillor was looking through the register of names of the people who worked in the sewage works and he came across the name McGlumpher.
    'Look at this chap – twenty years' service and never a day off. That's dedication for you. Doesn't even take a weekend off. Magnificent.' So they decide to go down and visit him and thank him for so many years of loyal service.
    There's McGlumpher down in the vaults happily singing away to himself . . . 'Sugar in the morning, Sugar in the evening, Sugar at supper time . . . She wore red feathers and a hula-hula skirt . . .'
    'Er . . . Good morning, Mr McGlumpher. We are most impressed by the way you've dedicated so much of your life to your work. How is it that you like it so much that you even give up your free time to do it?'
    'Well, it's fascinating, really. For instance, I can identify all those different jobbies – it's like bird-watching . . . See that one over there? That beige one?'
    'That one?'
    'No – that one there.'

'Aye.'

'That's a butcher's.'

'How can you possibly tell?'

'Well, all those little wood-shavings come from a butcher's floor . . . And that one there: that's a barber's. You can tell because of the wee bits of hair attached to it.'

'Good heavens, that really is fascinating.'

'And see that one just coming down the tunnel now – that long thin one?'

'Yes, yes.'

'That's my wife's.'

'Goodness gracious. How can you possibly know that?'

'Because it's got ma sandwich tied tae it.'

People tell me to keep my nose clean so I always do. Now I'm a showbiz personality, I pick it with a silver spoon. But I understand that crabs' claws are the ecologically sound way to do it.

Nose-pickers sometimes act like a persecuted minority. They behave in this very surreptitious way. For no good reason. Because, after all, nose-picking is an entirely classless activity and it can be enormous fun.

What always staggers me is that when people blow their noses they look into their hankies to see what came out. What do they expect to find? A silver sixpence?

One big worry in playing lots of different places is the electricity. That's one reason I've stuck to the acoustic guitar. I would hate to get an electric shock on stage: chrome-plated testicles . . . you run for a bus and you sound like an alarm clock going off. People call you jingle balls.

I suppose it's a good idea to keep fit if you're travelling. But personally I don't think I've broken into a run since I was about fourteen. I don't play many sports – I used to have a tennis racket but that was just for pretending to play the guitar with in front of the mirror when I was about twelve. You know that one – you always get caught by your big sister coming into the room and you feel daft. My sister now, because she's my sister, is always being asked why she's not funny. She's a teacher. So she says: 'Well, *he* doesn't teach kids and *I* don't tell jokes.'

Swimming and diving, though, I like. Once got done for drunken diving. I'm amazed at how seriously some people take it: we stayed at a hotel in Dubai where the American families were giving their kids points for diving, like they were in the Olympics or something . . . 'Very good, Bart, seven points' . . . all that sort of stuff.

Cycling's my favourite. The rules are simple: head down, arse up and bugger the lot at the back. We heard of this guy in Dubai who'd been cycling round the world – from Glasgow he was I think. And he hit on this neat dodge of hiding all his money in the handlebars so that no one would find it while he was asleep by the side of the road. Then someone nicked his bike.

Golf's one sport I've never got into, though I got a golfing joke from Jimmy Tarbuck . . .

Two blokes out on a golf course. One of them is carrying this black briefcase with him while they're playing.

'Eh, what's in that briefcase?'

'It's my tools . . . I'm a hitman for the Mafia.'

'Naw . . . *really*? Can I have a look?'

'Sure.'

Opens the briefcase and there inside is the whole works: rifle with telescopic sight, the lot.

'Can I take a look through the sight?'

'Sure.'

'Jeees . . . it's powerful isn't it? Look I can see my house through it. Wow . . . And there's my wife up in the bedroom . . . Wait a minute . . . There's that bastard from next door . . . And they're . . . Jesus. They're taking their clothes off! This is – Hey, how much do you charge?'

'Thousand pounds a shot.'

'Right. I'll give you two thousand. I want her shot through the head. And I want him shot through the balls. OK?'

So the hitman takes the rifle. Moves the sight a bit. Aims. Then moves very slightly. Adjusts the rifle again.

'Come on . . . hurry up . . . what are you playing at?'

'Steady on – I'm trying to save you a grand.'

Pole-vaulting's another thing that's passed me by. But I always wonder how these pole-vaulters get their pole to the competition. Do they hang it out of the bus window or what?

I've always wondered, too, what a Martian would make of football if he saw it. How would he describe it to another Martian? 'The object is to hit the goalkeeper with the ball as many times as you can. If you miss all your pals kiss you and you feel a right eejit.'

I watched the England versus Hungary game with a lot of players. They're funny, soccer-players. They all eat sweeties. Alan Ball would say: 'Have one of these, Bill,' and you get handed this enormous pink-and-nutty nougat. Yugh. I was there with Jimmy Tarbuck – remember him? – and when there was a goal we were both going to throw our pints of lager in the air and drop the glasses so that everyone would be soaked but no one would know who'd done it. Very grown up, eh?

Self defence for foreign parts is something you're meant to learn. When I was in the paras they had this delightful training game in which they tie your hands behind your back and make you fight – kicking, biting, butting.

But when we were in Bahrein I was doing this routine on stage about a Glasgow fight and doing lots of butting. And there were these Americans in the audience, oil people from Saudi, and they didn't know what I was doing. Then afterwards there were a lot of drunk expatriates throwing each other and tables into the pool, blood everywhere, and one Scottish bloke butted another right in front of the American couple and they went: 'So *that's* what he was on about'. Very educational for them.

One thing to remember in these hot climates is to go easy on the sun. I have this problem – when I take off my T-shirt to sunbathe people think I'm a milk bottle.

I have to be insured on all these trips. In fact I'm the proud owner of a plaque from Lloyds for the longest tour – eighty-one dates – without a claim. But you have to go through this medical beforehand, with a company doctor who wants to know if you drink and smoke and everything. 'Drink? Me? Oh, I have the occasional lager and lime after a game of squash . . . sometimes a glass of white wine with a meal . . . and maybe brandy in the Christmas cake, but that's about it.' And twenty-five cigarettes a day. I like smoking. I think we're a lot more likely to get blown away than to get cancer.

You have to pace yourself when you're performing all the time. I don't have intervals in my shows any more because I find it so difficult to get started up a second time. My sex life's much the same.

Oral sex seems to have become awfully popular – the only thing I don't like about it is the view. But, in fact, I think oral sex is really when your'e knackered – and you just talk about it.

ou can always tell the people who haven't flown before. They're in their smart gear. 'We're going on a plane so we'd better put on our best gear.' They see the wee button you press for the stewardess and they press it and talk into the wee air funnel... 'Eh, could we have some biscuits and two teas, please – and no sugar in one of the teas.'

The security men have a funny job. Running their hands up and down people's bodies all day. I like to say: 'Was it good for you, too?' when they've finished.

I love the paging system at airports. When I arrived in Los Angeles there was a message for a 'Mr Yassar Arafat... Mr Yassar Arafat ... white courtesy telephone please'. You'd have thought they'd have all hit the deck.

Once I got called over the loudspeaker at Hampden Park when my aunt died. They put out a loudspeaker announcement: 'Will Mr Billy Connolly please come to the administration office?' And when I got there, there were four other Billy Connollys there too. One of them was a midget and quite naturally he hated me because he was always being called Big Yin by his mates.

These life jackets they have under the seats – what are they for? It's not much use if you're heading for Manchester at 500 miles an hour. What do you do? Tell the pilot to aim for a puddle? But have you ever *seen* a life jacket on a plane? I don't believe they're actually there – I think they get nicked by those blokes who own wee boats.

Because I've been drinking usually before I get on the plane I always need a piss as soon as they bring the food round. So I always have to make the other two guys get up and they have to hold their trays and can't sit down because I've put my tray on one of their seats.

We had a very bumpy landing in Jersey. I hated it. Then Captain Carruthers comes on the blower: 'I'd like to apologise for the rather positive side of that landing.' Rather positive! I nearly broke my bloody back! What if I die, I was thinking? What if I die and go to hell – stuck in the same room as Ian Paisley for ever!

Flying over Utah we hit what they laughingly refer to as turbulence and I thought, God, I hope we don't go down here. I don't want the Mormons to handle my funeral. I was once in a plane that got struck by lightning when I was in the paras but that was OK – it hit a fuel tank and we had to stay on in Malta for an extra six days while they repaired it.

We had another fright leaving Tokyo to go to Los Angeles. One of those 'the-aircraft-will-be-returning-to-land-ladies-and-gentlemen' jobs. The engine has conked out or some such event.

Beside me was this Texas woman who was on her way back to America so that she could watch the royal wedding on the television there. And she kept saying: 'Well, as long as we get back in time for the exchanging of vows, I don't mind.' I was slightly more worried about the imminent possibility of a burial at sea but I suppose we all have different priorities.

Going over to America on the plane, I'm sitting next to this very large guy who eats every single thing on his tray: the roll, the shrimp salad, the casserole, the wee carrots, the croquet potatoes . . . And I'd ordered fish, being of vegetarian persuasion, but I didn't feel hungry so he asks me if he can have the fish as well. Sure. So he's got the fish with more potatoes and courgettes and salad. Then he has the biscuits and cheese and the trifle. Asks the stewardess if there's any more trifle. Of course. So he has some more trifle. Then the brandy and a couple of little chocolate mints. Then a coffee. And out of his jacket pocket he takes a wee packet of Sweet 'n' Low, the non-fattening sweetener, and pops them into his coffee . . .

Sweet 'n' Low is also what people in Hollywood call cocaine. It says here.

Airline food is the most extraordinary thing. It's on those funny trays that you can't tell where the food starts and the tray ends. I was on one plane – and you know you can now order a vegetarian meal beforehand – and this Indian bloke had ordered one and when the stewardess is going round with the food he shouts out: 'I'm the vegetable' to identify himself. I liked that.

But you don't get that on the wee planes – the ones where they have a whip-round for the pilot at the end of the trip. And they don't have all the wonderful things you get in the toilets with the big airlines – you try out all the aftershaves and come out smelling like you just fell into a rose bush. But in the economy class, the toilet's always outside.

(Fifty years ago there were no inside toilets in lots of the Glasgow tenements. So what used to happen if it was cold and late at night was people would do a wee jobbie in a newspaper and then throw it into the street. One night a bloke did that and hit a policeman – THUNK – smack on the face. Shit all over him. So he looks up at the tenement window with a light on and shouts: 'YE DIRTY BAS-TARD!' And a voice comes down: 'Who are ye callin' a dirty bastard – you with shite all over your face?')

But one thing I've never fathomed out is why the water in aeroplane toilets is always boiling? And why is there no safety belt in the toilet? Just because you're having a wee jobbie is no reason why you should be discriminated against, is it? And why do they have a blind in the toilet? Who's going to be looking in through the window at 10,000 feet up? You'd have to be a pretty determined pervert.

You see some weird things in those baggage collection places. When I was with a bunch of Scottish football fans in Munich for the World Cup in 1974, one of them had put a wee Hovis loaf with a label attached on that thing that goes round and round with your luggage on it. So there are all those big holdalls and cases and rucksacks and this tiny wee loaf going round and round.

I had a pal at school who, whenever he saw a plane going past in the sky, would say: 'Aye that'll be ma Uncle Bobby – Heyyyy! Uncle Bobby!' And give it a wave. His Uncle Bobby was probably in Barlinnie but his mother had told him he was a pilot . . . 'Aye, ye won't see your Uncle Bobby for a wee while, son, he's become a pilot . . .'

There were a lot of American airmen who left wee boys and girls behind them in Glasgow . . . You'd get these poor young lassies of sixteen sitting at windows in Partick waiting for the Three Wise Men to appear . . .

Bloke in Glasgow who's made a few bob and bought a wee plane, one of those wee Pipers. So one day he takes his pal for a wee spin round Loch Lomond – 'Fancy going up for a wee spin? Come back and have a pint after?' 'Aye, sure.' So they're up in the air having a whale of a time. Looping the loop and looking out of the window at the hills. Then it's time to go back to the airport. Suddenly – whoom – the pilot has a heart attack and keels over. And his pal's going: 'C' mawn, Alec, dinnae play games . . . Alec! For Christ's Sake!' Slapping his face, giving him the kiss of life, massaging his heart. Nothing. The bloke's copped it. So he's grabbing all the knobs and levers, trying to handle the plane, and he makes contact with the control tower: 'I need help up here – ma pal's just had a heart attack and died and I dinnae know how tae handle these things and . . . I think we're upside down!'

'What makes you think you're upside down?' asks the control tower.

'Because the shit's coming out of ma collar!'

Keeping pigeons has always been big in Glasgow and this pal of mine, Peter McDougall, was telling me about this pub in Greenock which is in quite a tough industrial area. This guy comes into the pub with his box with his pigeon in it. In Scotland they call pigeons 'doos' – so he had his wee doo in his box – and they get very close to them, quite fanatical about them. So he's had a few pints and he goes to the toilet and says to the next guy: 'Wull you watch ma doo fur me?' 'Oh, aye.' And the box is going wheishhh and moving around a bit so he goes: 'I'll just take a wee look at this.' Opens the box. Whifffff! The doo goes scudding along in the pub and settles on one of those mock-Tudor beams, one of those Formica things. The owner comes out of the toilet and sees it and goes: 'Awww, Christ . . .' and gets a wee tin with corn in it to tempt him down. But then a drunk comes out of the lavvie and shouts: 'Ah'll show ye how tae get it doon,' and gets a brush and goes WHACK! Feathers come drifting down and the doo has three heart attacks. So the owner of the pigeon goes over to the barman – really cool – 'Hey, John, could you phone for two ambulances, please.' 'Two?' 'Aye, one for the pigeon and the other for that *bastard*.'

① FILL POCKETS WITH HEAVY OBJEC

③ COVER UP WITH YOUR NATIONAL FLAG, ENSURING THAT ONE END IS DISCREETL NAILED TO THE GROUND.

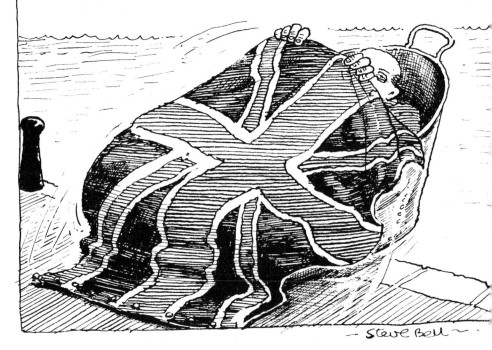

— Steve Bell —

2) LIE IN ZINC BATH POSITIONED WITH BACK OVERHANGING THE SEA OF YOUR CHOICE:

4) PERFORM BACKWARD ROLL INSIDE BATH...

5) ...WHICH SLIDES GRACEFULLY BENEATH WAVES.

THE SEA

he sea should be avoided at all costs or just glimpsed at from the first-class cabin of a jumbo jet – just to make sure you've got to where you're going to. It's far too cold and wet and dangerous and it takes up too much room. Does it really need twice as much room as the land or is it just being greedy?

Still, it has its uses. We found it very handy for cleaning the dog. What we would do in Drymen was throw a stick into the loch, the dog would go after it and bring it back – because it knew that was what was expected of dogs – then we would put shampoo on it and throw the stick back in again. Perfect. (I used to have to clean the cat, too, but I gave it up – all that hair on your tongue.)

My earliest memories of the sea were going fishing on the Clyde. And something that happens to every Glasgow dad would happen – a Durex would come floating downstream. 'Dad, Dad – what's this? Is it a trout, Dad?' 'Put that *doon!*' 'But, Dad . . .'

When I was at school, I saw all those Esther Williams films with her swimming underwater and smiling and looking elegant. So I used to practise in the baths in Glasgow, struggling along under water, trying to smile. People kept rescuing me.

When I started out as an apprentice in the shipyards, I was terrified of all the older blokes. They used to say to me: 'Go and get this and fetch that,' and I'd do it. And one time they said: 'Can you go fetch this frae the Stowaway's Locker?' So off I went. 'Eh – excuse me, could you tell me where the Stowaway's Locker is?' 'Aye, son, doon there, turn right, keep on past the paintshop and you'll see it.' Off again. 'Er . . . is this the Stowaway's Locker, please?' 'Naw, son – doon past thae benches there, turn left and ask again.' The place never existed, of course. It was all a big joke at the expense of the apprentices. So after I'd been there a few months one of them asked me to fetch some carborundum, which you have for sanding stuff down. And I thought: 'Carborundum' – that doesn't sound real. It must be another of their wee jokes. So I said; 'Naw, cannae fool me this time.' They didn't know what I was on about.

Another time, one of the welders sent an apprentice off to get him twenty Embassy tipped. 'Aye, OK – what if they don't have any?'

'Och, just get me anything, son.' He came back with two hot pies.

I was going to be in this pirate movie and play the part of a Scottish engineer. But, of course, they had no engines in those days so he didn't have a lot to do (it's like one of those great jobs you put yourself down as when you don't want to be taken off the broo – sheepdog handler in Shepherd's Bush, engineer on a private ship. Or, like a pal of mine did, sign on as a welder in a place like Blairgowrie, which is bloody miles from the sea and has no call for anyone except berry-pickers and probably only has a stream running through it at the very most.) And this engineer was meant to be very superstitious, so he was always throwing things overboard. A woman? Bad luck. Overboard. He finds the last dodo in existence and throws it overboard because it's bad luck.

The power-boat champion of Great Britain lives near my house in Drymen, Lady Arran. She's about sixty-eight and goes bounding down the loch at a few hundred miles an hour. Anyway, she keeps all those strange animals on her land – kangaroos and llamas. One night the local poachers were on her patch – the Invergraw Grouse Beaters everyone calls them – and they were camping out, into the wine and everything, when one of them looks out of the tent and sees a kangaroo! His mates wouldn't believe him.

I met these people in Doha who had a routine whereby they would wave at passing ships that were too far away to hear them and they would shout: 'Anyone not wearing knickers – wave!' And, sure enough, the punters on the other ships – not being able to hear a damn word – would wave back.

There's a club at Innerleithen near Loch Lomond, an anglers' club with a bar where I often meet up with people. It opens early for the boys. So we go into the bar, have a pint, then up onto the loch. And there's a bridge you have to go under before you get into the loch.

On this particular day, sitting on the bridge was the local drunk leaning over and watching all the boats go out. Apparently he had once been a splendid fisherman, a great angler, and he must have thought: 'Oh, I'd love tae go fishin' today . . .' because he was gazing at the boats. And through this alcoholic mist – he was in the old-Army-coat-drinking-Brasso-sleeping-in-doorways stage – he

47

must have decided to try to get out on the loch. Because he came down off the bridge and was swaying about on the bank, trying to hitch a lift in one of the boats.

And one of the boys in the boat says: 'Hey, wait a minute, that's John So-and-so, why don't we take him out with us?' 'Why not?' So they take him on board and he's well pleased. And they were doing trawling – not the Aberdeen kind but the kind where you just put the rods out behind you. It's very pleasant. The engine goes phut-phut-phut and you just sit there.

Anyway, the two guys who owned the boat worked for Ballantine's whisky distillery. And they had a little take-away with them. Three bottles of nippie sweetie. The man's all for it.

'Aye, gie's a wee one. There's one for the first fish. Here we go. All the best! Here's one for the open sea.' 'We're on a loch, John.' 'Och, never mind – here's one for the biggest wave. Here's one for eff-all . . . Down the face. Here we go.' So after half an hour of this he was well into it.

But it must have mixed very badly with the stuff he had been drinking the night before. Something is going on inside him. He has to lean over the side to be sick. He's giving it lots of Hughie and Ralph : 'HUGHHHEEE!! RAAAAALPHHH!!' Until there's nothing left and he can't be sick any more . . . so he's just doing those barking noises – 'HWOWHWOWHO!'

Now in the middle of all this puking – his teeth fall out. Splash. Into the loch. 'Aw, Jesus Christ! Ma teeth fell into the loch! Ma teeth fell in!'

'Sit down, sit down, for Christ's sake,' go the Ballantine's blokes, 'you'll have us all over! Sit down!' So they bundle him off to the front of the boat and he sits there in a wee huddled ball, mumbling and farting and burping.

So the two guys with the boat say: 'Now don't you worry – we'll find your teeth.' Loch Lomond is twenty-five miles long and God knows how deep but anyway they're going to have a look for them. So they turn the boat around and go: 'Can you see them there, Tam?' 'Naw, naw . . . is that them?' 'Don't think so . . . keep looking!'

Then finally when the wino's so out of it he doesn't notice, one of the pair winds the line in, takes the bait off and puts his own false teeth on the end. And he goes: 'Hey, Willie! Look – I've found John's teeth!' 'I don't believe it – would you credit that!'

And the drunk takes them. He's pleased and delighted. Tries them

48

on. 'Naw – they're no' mine.' And he throws them back into the loch.

Underwater swimming is something I got into in Barbados; not the aqualung, just the wee snorkel because the sea there is as clear as a bell. You swim around under water and these wee fish in incredible colours – turquoise and screaming crimson – come towards you in bunches of about seven million. Then I saw *Jaws*. After that, whenever I saw the wee fish going zing off to the right or the left all of a sudden, I would think: they must know something I don't know and they're not telling me. Must be a shark – not that there is a damn shark in the place but your imagination runs riot . . . you see your flipper following you and have a coronary.

But I love fishing. It's like transcendental meditation with a punch-line.

However, I think it's time they changed some of the ways of fishing – I'm all in favour of putting on a crash helmet, wading into the stream and nutting the salmon as they leap.

If Idi Amin ever dies, they'll bone him and send his skin over as a wetsuit for Cyril Smith.

— Steve Bel

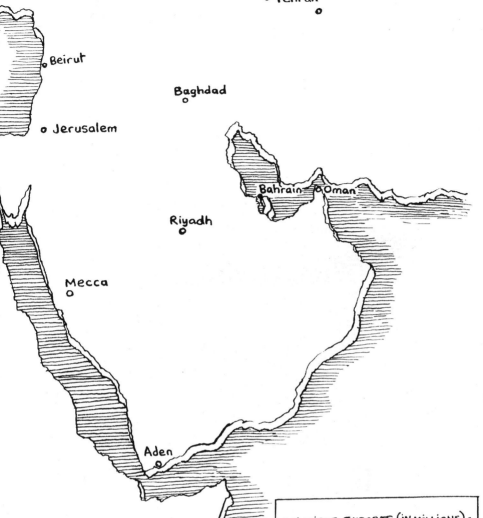

o Tehran
o

o Beirut

Baghdad
o

o Jerusalem

Bahrain o o Oman

Riyadh
o

Mecca
o

Aden
o

PRINCIPLE EXPORTS (IN MILLIONS):

 RELIGION

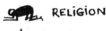 OIL

 CAMELS

MIDDLE EAST

The sun hasn't quite set on the British Empire as far as a lot of the punters out in the Middle East are concerned. It's hard for them out there. They come from a breed that once belonged to an Empire, run by an Emperor. Then it became a kingdom, run by a king. Now it's a country, run by a bunch of eejits. Some of them are amazingly patriotic – you can get quite a hostile reaction when you make jokes about the Queen Mother.

A lot of the old-timers who've been out there for ages are great – they love the people and the country and the language and they appreciate all the amazing things going on around them and don't imagine that they're superior in any way. But some of the new lot are a pain in the arse – they call the Arabs 'ragheads' and 'clothheads' and tell you all the time how stupid they are: if the Arabs are so stupid what does that make the people who work for them?

You get very tired of hearing how dirty the locals are. Some of the blokes won't go out with a woman if she's had an Arab boyfriend: 'I won't put my willie where a wog's willie's been,' and all that crap. And they call the rich Arabs 'jinglies' because they wear jewellery and dance in the discos.

Still, it's nice to see such well-oiled customers. For a lot of them out there it's 'Fantasy Island'. They're all in *True Brit*, starring John Wayne. They can invent whatever past they like for themselves so you keep meeting people who've played for Arsenal or Celtic and blokes who've had their own companies in England. Usually it's absolute crap, but why not if it makes them happy?

And they all give themselves such funny titles: you meet a welder from Govan and he calls himself 'an engineering consultant'. And a Brit! 'Hi – I'm one of the Brits.' Just off the plane from Govan and he's suddenly become a 'Brit'. Plumbers become 'hydraulic advisers'.

Unions are one topic they love out there. They go on about how the unions are ruining Britain – then in the next breath they tell you they have to go to bed because they're working Saturdays. There isn't a union in Britain that would agree to a six-day week. They tell you that the Arabs don't do any manual work except with the Spanish

52

waiter. They've got this thing that the Arabs must be gay because they have this very nice habit of holding hands as they stroll along.

A lot of them never bother to learn about the food or the language – they call the Emir the 'Emu' and tell you that the papers have to get permission to use any adjective to describe a member of the royal family. Which is not so different to what happens in Britain.

The language they use is great, though: 'AC' is 'air conditioning' – and I couldn't understand why 'AC' featured so much in their lives . . . and they're all either 'expats' or 'Brits'. And because bacon is banned in some parts of the Middle East it's become an under-the-counter sort of thing for which the code word is 'breakfast meat'.

They do get very homesick, though. In one of my stories at the show in Dubai I mentioned Buchanan Street station in Glasgow and there was a great cheer. Well, they can reload and fire again. No one in Glasgow wants it. Sometimes I think I could just read a road map of Scotland and it'd go down well. 'Falkirk' (Cheers) . . . 'Larkhall' (Hoooray) . . . 'Largs' (Yeeeaaahhh).

(I was with Matt McGinn in Buchanan Street station once and we were going up the stairs and there was a bunch of Rangers supporters coming down, well pissed. So there we are and I'm trying desperately hard not to look like a Catholic and Matt shouts at them: 'You're a dirty bunch of Orange Fenians!' and the poor buggers didn't know what to do.)

Another big number out there is videos, because there's so little in the way of entertainment. So everyone's after borrowing the latest Clint Eastwood or *French Connection*. The naughty ones to have are *Death of a Princess* which gets smuggled in under some other title, or *Deep Throat*. And the new ones on the circuit are called 'newies'.

Sex is quite big there. I think there must be an awful lot of wife-swapping and stuff going on. You keep seeing people with 'I Got Laid In The Gulf' and a picture of oil pipes on their T-shirts. And there's lots of innuendo and double entrendre flying about in the air: 'Sit on my knee and we'll see if something comes up.' Quite strange. Anyone who sleeps around publicly and doesn't mind who knows is called a 're-tread' and there are all sorts of stories about air hostesses, most of them untrue I'm sure.

Watching the guys at the pool you get the impression you should get one of those pairs of underpants that have a powderpuff in them – the Mandingo look.

Bahrein's the place you hit first when you come out from Britain, though they don't encourage tourists. There are hundreds of blokes out there working on the oil or in engineering and most of them don't bring their wives or girlfriends. So when a woman appears in the swimming pools there she doesn't need a towel after a swim – she gets dried by the heavy breathing.

The one thing they have to watch is drunken driving because the Arabs have, quite rightly, a big thing about foreigners running them over. But the well-connected ones have these 'get-out-of-jail-free' cards if they've got some connection with someone high up. I gather the prison is run by a Scot who does it as a hobby . . . Nice hobby to have. Yes, you have to watch it – tell a dirty joke and you lose a finger.

They do make a load of money though. The last time but one I met some Fifers who were working out there, making a fortune. They were so anxious not to spend any of it that they went to bed at eight p.m. so that they weren't tempted by the booze.

And do some of them drink out there when they've not seen it for a while! You get them telling you how primitive the Arabs are for pissing in the street and then you see them three hours later, plastered, throwing up in the car park . . .

You can get a drink in the hotels in Bahrein which you can't in Saudi Arabia, which is the next one down. So you get these born-again drunks arriving from Riyadh to spend the weekend getting out of it at the Holiday Inn. Some of them get so excited at seeing booze again after two months that they don't get past the duty-free place at the airport.

Then they hit the swimming pool and throw each other in, then they throw the women in. And the great joke was to announce over the hotel loudspeaker that Moshe Dayan was wanted in the foyer. Some of the guys have been there for years – they're usually those loners with awful marriages somewhere in the south of England – and they describe themselves as 'lifers'. But every two months they blow it all – we met blokes who'd spent more than two hundred pounds on the weekend just in booze – so they never earn enough to go back and start all these restaurants and things they say they're going to do.

Saudi Arabia's still regarded as the strictest place round there. We were having a drink with two Texans on their way back there after the weekend in Bahrein. They were having a couple of beers, which is forbidden back in Saudi, and saying they felt like Caryl Chessman must have felt before he went to the electric chair.

But we saw one bloke from Saudi who was wearing this T-shirt which had on it: 'Saudi Arabia Campaign For Real Ale', which I suppose is a bit like the Vatican Atheists' Society or the Barlinnie Hang-Gliding Club – they have arrows on the wings.

Women aren't allowed to drive cars there and there are very few western women so one popular joke is a bloke holding his willy in his hand and the willy's saying: 'Sorry, I've got a headache tonight.'

But Saudi Arabia is so rich that they can afford to go surf-boarding through the sand on Renoirs.

Das Island in the Gulf is even weirder though. There are no women there at all and they dress up for dinner so as not to let the standards slip. There's a great gay bloke who looks after the gardens, does it beautifully, so they gave him a wee team to help out and they're known as the Queen's Park Rangers. They have a five-star restaurant with furniture from Harrods.

The first thing you notice when you arrive in Dubai is the colour of the grass at the airport – I think they should roll it up and smoke it. I love it there – we've stayed a couple of times at the Metropolitan hotel which is so called because it's miles from the city and the market, which is fantastic. They've got a newsagent's at the hotel called W. H. Myth – honest. And the people working there are really friendly; they call me Billyconnolly as though it was all one word: 'Hello, Billyconnolly, did you have a good trip?'

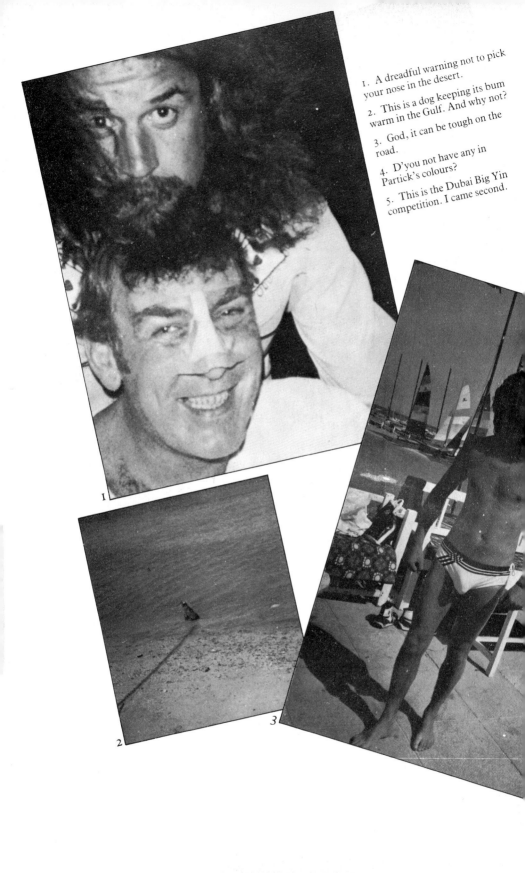

1. A dreadful warning not to pick your nose in the desert.

2. This is a dog keeping its bum warm in the Gulf. And why not?

3. God, it can be tough on the road.

4. D'you not have any in Partick's colours?

5. This is the Dubai Big Yin competition. I came second.

1

2

3

4

5

One of the waiters at the hotel, an Indian bloke, was telling us about the drinking system there. You have to earn a certain amount before you get a drinks permit. I bet Mrs Thatcher would love to introduce something like that in Britain to keep the workers in hand.

They put a bottle of Scotch in my room, which was nice of them but I didn't drink it so when I left I gave it to the waiter. And the guy on the door, a great big Pakistani with a Jimmy Edwards moustache, checked when I left that it was OK for them to have the bottle. So I said sure, and he said: 'Well, we'll have a wee dram tonight, sir.'

There's a disco in the hotel run by a fellow who used to run the Valbonne in London. But it's quite odd because it's all this red and black furniture and strobe lighting and the latest hits and everything – and fifty blokes all staring at the one woman who's dancing. One night we were there and there were only four women the whole evening, stewardesses I think they were, and we said: 'Is it always as imbalanced as this?' And they said: 'What do you mean, this is a good night!' I had a dance with a Texan's wife who we'd been chatting to and suddenly you realise that there's fifty pairs of eyes staring at you. It certainly makes you a wee bit self-conscious about your dance steps.

The pool at the Metropolitan has a wee sign beside it saying: 'Will patrons kindly refrain from running, pushing, jumping and petting.'

I always perform at the Country Club in Dubai – open air with a big stage and the drapes are all in that Thailand whorehouse red colour.

The last time I did a dinner spot for the club members and there was a woman from Glasgow who kept interrupting my jokes. I couldn't believe it – she kept butting in just before the punchline. I said I'd go to her house at three in the morning and ruin her timing. It had no effect.

The punters from Saudi Arabia have their own illicit hooch – sidiki or sid, they call it . . . People say I'm a lush because they see me drinking wine. But I'm not a lush – Jesus drank wine and no one accused him of being a lush. The main beer they drink there is Amstel, which is what they put on cuts where I come from.

Some of the expats are a laugh. A lot are ex-services types who must like that sort of barrack-room life. They were all ex-army boxing champs. Not that I've ever met someone who boxed in the army who *wasn't* a champ. It seems that there was no one who boxed in the services and just got blootered. But we heard one of the expats complaining about the Arabs and saying: 'Aye, the Arabs are as bad as Jews.' They are all much wealthier than they could hope to be in England but they still complain a lot – some of them will just not be happy as long as their arse looks at the ground.

One popular rumour is that the local sheik has a sort of pleasure dome built underneath his palace – a whole Disneyland. I've no idea if it's true or not but there is an amazing place called Leisureland outside Dubai – it's got swings made like giant bananas, enormous cherries that eat you up if you go inside them and pineapples that shower you with water.

The security bloke there is George Haddad who is about seven foot six, a great big gentle bloke who looks like Jaws from the James Bond films. He's looked after himself and he's perfectly proportioned – watching him dance in the disco is great because he's so light on his feet.

And out at the Leisureland place they have this enormous ice-rink which all the Arabs skate on – you get this wonderful sight of everyone in floor-length dishdashs skimming around the rink with rock music playing in the background.

The money thing's big there. People keep going on about some thirteen-year-old Arab prince gets given five million pounds by his dad, but the Prince of Wales was given half of Mayfair and a bit of Cornwall just for arriving on the scene.

I'm now Honorary President of the Sharjah Formation Bum-Biting Team. They have a routine whereby two of the team kneel on the ground beside some unsuspecting soul, link hands and try to bite his bum. Thighs don't count. And there's an underwater biting association attached to it.

We were there during their most severe winter – at night you had to wear a cardigan to go out. Still, they've given us some great songs: 'Dubai, Don't Cry . . .'

Abu Dhabi is a bit of a funny one – I don't like it as much as Dubai and Doha. We performed at the club there – it used to be the British Club but it has to be a wee bit less British now; and it's another place where you can only drink with permission. When we arrived there someone was just about to be executed for robbing a petrol station. Adultery means a stoning – we wanted to know if we saw any adultery taking place on the telly in our hotel whether it was OK to stone the screen.

We had to perform indoors there; it was to have been on the tennis courts but the tennis-players wouldn't allow it – I hope they all have coronaries.

But the drive through the desert to Abu Dhabi is magnificent and they've built their own forest, too – it's all drip–fed by some amazing system. When you get into the town itself, the first thing that hits you is this burst of colour, if that's what colour does when it comes unexpectedly on the scene – all those very jolly brightly-coloured flowers and bushes which they've made a great effort to get growing there.

The other side of it is that they're building so fast that the whole of the town is like a building site and you're for ever falling down holes in the middle of the pavement. But that's OK.

The DJ's you meet there, who work on the English-language radio stations, are all from the south of England and Australia – they get these shiny Thai bomber jackets with their names embroidered on the back of them: the kind of jacket you wear when you get off the plane at Heathrow and you know your friends are going to be meeting you.

Abu Dhabi's a place you have to watch the booze as well – if the locals get drunk they get a flogging . . .

The Sheiks there aren't short of a few bob – some of them are as rich as Elton John. And they've made sure that the locals all get a house and some money which is quite a smart move. I love the noises there – the faithful being called to prayer in the evening. And the names of some of the wee shops you see: the Shaheed Coolbar Teastall and the Up-To-Date Tailors.

The place I played at in Doha is this new theatre they just built up from scratch thanks mainly to one woman there called Jenny who was determined to get it going – it's right in the middle of the desert, all around looks like a place where old tyres go to die – but it's an amazing achievement and it's a great wee place to perform. The tour was originally called 'Bite Yer Bum' but it was changed to 'On Yer Bike' for the Middle East because it was reckoned to be a bit rude.

When they did a panto there they had to cut out certain words so as not to offend – you couldn't mention the desert. But I've never had any problems there. (I love panto – I had a pal who was playing one of the ugly sisters in Cinderella and got him to put cans of McEwan's in his hair instead of rollers.)

And another nice thing about it is that Doha has remained much more Arab than some of the other places around, which I like.

They have a club called The Falcon Club or The Pigeon Club depending on what you feel about the blokes in it. Falcons are a big deal out there, a lot of Arabs have them and the expats get very pissed off when they get onto a plane with one on their arm because the expats aren't allowed to take their cats with them.

Doha is still in the middle of being built – it's all concrete and sand and makes Govan look like Las Vegas. It's such a funny name: Dough–Ha! It even sounds like a hole in the ground. Another place name I love out there is Daran. It sounds like it should be pronounced *Daran!* – like *Daran-tara!*

The desert is amazing. I love it deeply though sometimes you wonder what you're doing there – sand in your porridge and every time you blow your nose it's as if the chimney had just been swept. It didn't do my split ends a lot of good either.

I've done 'Desert Island Discs', a helluva good idea for a programme. Roy Plomley was saying that he did it first as a trial for the BBC and he had eleven well-known friends so he just used them and that was sixty-seven years ago now. It's great, though there's some records you wouldn't choose – in LA I heard a four-minute tape of a bloke with diarrhoea going for a crap. It was perfect in every detail, the footsteps running to the bathroom, the zip, that spl-ll-aaa-tttt. Then that sigh of relief – Ohhhhh! Then some more . . . . Beeeeppppp. Still, it's not quite the sort of thing for 'Desert Island Discs'.

The camels are wonderful. You see them strolling around like they owned the place. And you have to give way for them on the roads on the ground that they were there before the motor car, which is a nice concept. The only thing is – they're a bit niffy. But just seeing them takes you into a whole different world – 'Ah, the heat and the flies . . . and the people . . . Have that boy washed and bring him to my tent.'

What you have to watch out for in the deserts – apart from all the expats masturbating – are the flying beetles. They're kamikazes, don't care if you kill them as long as they hit their targets. And if you see a wee one you can't relax because it's probably just out scouting for its big brother.

I like the whole Arab world a lot. But the thing is if you say you like Arabs people automatically think that you don't like Jews which is completely untrue.

And the lovely thing about travelling out there is what you see when you wake up in the morning – you look out of your window and see these beautiful dhows, which is a bit of a change from what you see out of a hotel window in Ipswich or Birmingham.

I don't know whether there's anything in it at all but somehow there seem to be a lot of Scottish things that overlap with the Arab world – like the pipes which they have out there. I wanted to get a tartan top to the outfit I bought. Look like a North Sea Oil Sheik. The headdresses are great – and they use the rope bit for hobbling the camels at night. And it's funny when you think about it that all the religions that have made it big come from this area – Moses, Jesus, Mohammed.

The nicest thing is when you see dishdashs in the audience and get Arabs coming up afterwards who've enjoyed the show. Sometimes you get one who's all kitted out who's been to Strathclyde University or something, doing engineering, and he's got a Scottish accent.

I heard someone on the radio talking about his trip to the Holy Land. He'd asked the cab driver to take him to Calvary and he'd been told: Calvary's a one way street.'

Iran is the one place in the area I haven't been invited to but I don't lose a lot of sleep at night through not being able to go there at the moment . . . when I played the Ayatollah on 'Not the Nine O'Clock News' it was the night that the Iranian Embassy was on fire and they postponed it on grounds of good taste – but when was 'Not the Nine O'Clock News' meant to be good taste?

Cairo was one place I visited, to do a St Andrew's dinner, which was a real treat. You get all the different nationalities out there, a lot of them working in construction. So there's Americans, Germans, Canadians – and all the countries celebrate their Thanksgiving or national day or whatever and invite the other nationalities along. The Scots hadn't had anything before so they decided to throw a St Andrew's Night in aid of the Cairo Scottish Country Dance Society.

Sadat's interpreter was sitting next to me at the table. I did Mustapha – it's a Syrian tune – on the banjo and the waiters were all dancing. It was a long way from Falkirk.

They were a nice bunch, none of that Uncle Jock thing about them. They were wearing kilts and drinking Athol Brose – malt whisky, oatmeal and cream – which I have never had before. It's lethal. Sneaks up on you. You have three or four and suddenly your knees don't work and there's a lot of hooching and heeching.

The Egyptians are so nice. We only had a week there so we couldn't go down the Valley of the Kings. I just stayed around the pyramids, which was plenty.

Everyone was friendly – they don't want to fight. A lot of things fell into place about the Six-Day War. They just don't give a monkey's – I suppose that's why they build these useless things like pyramids. That's the answer to youth unemployment – let's make lots of pyramids and silly things.

1. Hilary Thomas, a young Australian physiotherapist en route for the Royal Wedding in London asks for an autograph in Bahrein. (Eh?)

2. What is the Bahrein Dead Cat Society? Ask any damn cat in Bahrein.

3. Good morning.

4. A bazaar experience in the Middle East.

THE BAHRAIN DEAD CAT SOCIETY

5. They never said anything about this in the Bert Weedon song book.

6. We were going to make a feeble joke about zebras crossing but decided against it at the last moment.

7. Another bazaar experience.

Remember when Mark Thatcher got lost in the desert on that motor rally? My dad was saying that he was expected up at Linwood because his mother had made a desert there, too.

Sherlock Holmes used to say to Dr Watson that before anyone could talk, they would communicate with each other by music and that's why music has such a hold on you, it takes you back to the days when you couldn't talk to each other.

Not that that's any bloody help when you're trying to get a cup of tea and you don't know the language. I don't have too massive a command of languages but I caught one way to get around in Arabic countries which is 'IBM'. That stands for Inchalal, Bukra and Malish.

Inchalal means 'god willing'. Bukra means 'tomorrow' and Malish means 'welllll, mmm, you never know your luck'. Those three will get you through quite a bit. The other one is Hamdulalal which is the best way to say you're feeling great. It means 'God is looking down on me.' If someone asks you how you're feeling and you say that and look like you mean it, then you've got yourself a friend. It's like cracking a safe.

But language is fascinating. The real names for things can be so awful in English. Like 'penis' and 'scrotum'. Yugh. No wonder they had to invent different words for them like willies and bums and tits.

I love those wee boys in Glasgow that you hear who've just learnt how to swear but they can't do it properly so they go: 'You – you – fuck bugger jobbies . . . aye, and underpants, too!'

It's weird that people still say in the papers that audiences can't understand what I'm saying – I was telling the audience at the Cambridge Theatre that I couldn't believe that people still found me hard to understand and they all went: 'What?'

As for all the different currencies, the best idea is to have a roadie who handles it all for you. In the Middle East the currency is dirhams, or 'heedrum hodrums' as they're popularly known.

The other alternative is to rob a bank, which is something I've always wanted to do just once. I reckon I could get away with it by shaving off my beard, doing the robbery, pissing off until the beard had grown again and then coming back. No one would ever believe it, would they? It's the sort of *Rififi* bank job that appeals.

The great scam at airports is that long-term car park racket: a bloke goes into the airport, steals a car from the car park, takes it into town – any town – says he has to sell it quickly because he's going abroad. Sells it. Then he steals it back because he's got a copy of the key. Takes it back to the airport and puts it back in the parking place so that it's ready for the guy coming back from abroad.

Ah, well, as the old Arabic saying has it: 'Long may the sand fly up your jacksie.'

And half a camel is better than quarter a budgie.

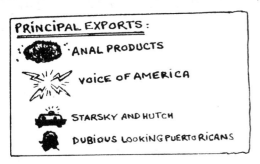

PRINCIPAL EXPORTS:

ANAL PRODUCTS

VOICE OF AMERICA

STARSKY AND HUTCH

DUBIOUS LOOKING PUERTO RICANS

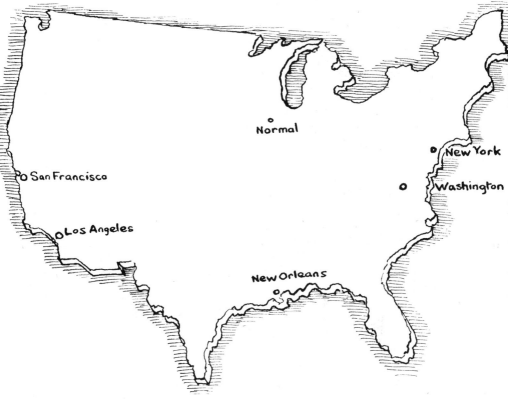

Normal

New York

San Francisco

Washington

Los Angeles

New Orleans

AMERICA

eople always say that America is really violent and particularly New York. But Glasgow's not all that tame. I never get mugged in New York because I look like another mugger. And I always get an elevator to myself because no one will come in and join me, because I remind them of Charles Manson.

But America is still the land of opportunity. There was a Glasgow boy called Bob Dick who went out to Philadelphia and became a bagman for the Mafia. Ended up marrying the boss's wife. A real Glasgow boy who'd had this really adventurous life . . . the dream of the Scottish hardmen.

I remember one hardman in Glasgow called Colly Beattie. You didn't call him Colly. It was Mr Beattie. And to meet him was like meeting a film star. A real event in your life.

Jimmy Boyle, who I've visited in Barlinnie and who's a friend now, was a complete hardman. And it's odd meeting him now and thinking of him like that, when he does these beautiful, gentle sculptures.

I watch a lot of television in America. Twenty-four hours of guaranteed crap. It's wonderful. I just sit there with my cheeseburger and my beer on the shag-pile carpet and watch all these extraordinary programmes.

The commercials are the best. You get a lot of medical adverts – I suppose it's because of their medical system. I think it's called 'a rip-off'.

They have ads for diarrhoea sufferers: 'Diarrhoea is no laughing matter.' I'd love to see the guy coming on . . . 'Good evening, ladies and gentlemen. I'm here to conduct an appeal on behalf of the sufferers of chronic diarrhoea. Not many people realise that . . . oh . . . er . . . excuse me . . . I'll be right back.' Exit with the bum-tightly-closed walk. That would be much more effective.

There are a lot of fairly boring ones too. Those 'every-record-ever-made' for a dollar type of offers, like they used to have with K-tel in Britain.

Everything that Slim Whitman ever sang for anybody who likes anything that Slim Whitman ever sang. Or those Italian ones – Guiseppe Connello's Greatest Hits. It's the smallest record in the world. Probably the singing telegram he sent his mother on Mother's Day. A selection of Polish waltzes. Who buys them? Some bampot in an attic who's into Polish waltzes, I suppose.

They have another one where this motherly-looking soul comes on – you instinctively know that she makes great apple pies . . . Mom – spelt the same each way, turn it upside down and it spells WOW . . . that sort of person . . . Anyway she comes on with that powdery face like a soda scone and says: 'Why don't you show your loved ones that you really love them? Buy the plot yourself before you go.' And they advertise coffins as well, except they call them caskets. They've got the whole works: Sony stereo, and a phone inside it probably.

You get an amazing picture of what's important to people in Los Angeles just by watching the commercials there: loads of ads for alcoholic dry-out places and drug clinics, lawyers to draw up claims for you and a lot about God and cavities both of which seem to be important on the West Coast. And lots of ads for nice cosy wee psychiatric hospitals where you can ditch the relatives.

But my favourite ad was for Preparation H, a haemorrhoid ointment. They come on the telly and say: 'For your haemorrhoidal problems . . .' and I thought Oh, yes, because, as the Scottish press always says, I have an anal fixation. I just happen to think bums are funny. So they show you the tube of Preparation H. And I think: OK America, how are you going to handle *this* one? Surely there isn't going to be a big pink bum on the screen? No such luck . . .

We find ourselves in the middle of a party. People are dancing to records and looking very happy and smiling. And they're very well-preserved. The guys are definitely not plumbers or shipyard workers. They have a good tan. And the women all have that complexion that looks like a cowboy boot. They're all wearing Crimplene – those terrible trouser suits: the arse is hanging out but the crease is still there. The men have this disturbing American habit of wearing white belts and shoes so they look like Cindy Dolls. They've all got teeth like the Osmonds.

(I have this enduring fantasy that there is *another* Osmond. But they never talk about him because he's terribly decadent and a junkie and lives in a house where even the soap is dirty. And they're all terrified that one day someone will discover it and tell the *National Enquirer* about it. And I bet his teeth are yellow and rotten.)

Well . . . it's a middle-class house – what Americans call a home.

Nobody has a house in America, they've all got 'homes'. 'You've got a wonderful *home*' . . . you could live in a septic tank and they'd still say: 'You've got a wonderful *home* – I want you to know, George, that this is one beautiful home.'

They're dancing away – the safe kind of dancing, not the Hot Gossip stuff. And they're dancing to this very safe record – something like Des O'Connor without the screaming guitars.

(I was telling someone about this in Bahrein. It was very reassuring that no one laughed when I mentioned Des O'Connor which must mean that no one's heard of Des O'Connor there . . . They've heard of Max Boyce there – he's about as funny as a burning orphanage . . . people always wonder how I go off at tangents as though it's all a carefully plotted thing but the truth is that I've got such terrible powers of concentration that I can only stick with one thing for about three minutes and then I wander off and have to come back. I think it's something to do with growing up in the presence of radio and television – you're used to only concentrating as far as the commercial breaks, and then taking a breather and I think my mind's got to that state that it has to keep changing the subject.)

Anyway. I'm still sitting there with my cheeseburger wondering how they're going to get round to haemorrhoids . . .

I had not long to wait. The main guy, a sort of Clark Gable character, Mr Smoothie . . . suddenly goes: 'Ohhhh!' – still dancing though. And his wife says: 'What's wrong, George?' And he says: 'I don't feel so good, Dolores.' Then she comes out with the legend: 'Are your haemorrhoids playing you up, George?' Poor George – I Took My Piles To the Party and Some Bugger Asked Me To Dance.

Well . . . I'm out of my simulated leather chair at this point. I couldn't handle it. Spat my cheeseburger all over the wall and spilled my beer into my crutch and now I'm sitting on the shag-pile with my head where my arse used to be. And the carpet's one of those kind that give you electric shocks: you go to switch the telly on and you go straight out like a flag.

So I'm looking at the guy thinking: so he's got haemorrhoids – that can't be fun – but why is he holding his forehead? I mean, I know everything's bigger in America but . . . And then my mind shot back to Glasgow and the shipyards where I used to work and all those big bears that used to work there. They always used to sound like dogs fighting when they were talking to each other. 'Waheyehheeh, uhhwufff . . .'

And when I was an apprentice there – when I was all plukey with a face like a butcher's window – they always used to say: 'Hey, don't sit there, you'll get piles.' I had no idea what they meant. I was always looking for a little pile of something that would disappear up your jacksie.

The amount of times they talked about it, a lot of them must have had haemorrhoids. And I wondered how the big Glasgow bear would have dealt with it . . . He wouldn't be at no dance in no Crimplene trousers. He would be sitting at home reading the sports pages. Belt and braces on – very security-conscious race the Scots. And he'd say: 'Hey, Senga,' (which is Agnes backwards in case you didn't know), 'Hey, Senga, ma piles are gie'in' me jip. Look out the wire brush and Dettol, will ye?' But back to the party . . . They go off to the bathroom. Because he can't apply it himself. Because bums are in such awkward positions, all tucked away in the corner. Mind you, your own bum never looks like your bum in the mirror either – 'That's no ma bum! I've got a tight wee bum,' you think to yourself . . .

Whatever they're doing in the bathroom, they get done because they're back at the party, and he's dancing again. He does a lot of bumwork to show how successful it's been. Because when he walked out he was like a giraffe having a drink. I would have loved to do an advert for the British market. So I did write off to Preparation H in England. They wrote back: Sod off, pervert.

The TV news in America is quaint. More like a variety show. It's all: 'Helllooo and now over to Bob . . . Thanks, Bob, and here's Mandy.' I watched the royal wedding in Los Angeles which is something I don't think I'd have watched in England, but there's something about watching it at three a.m. on Sunset Boulevard. He said.

When you fly from Australia to Los Angeles, you arrive about two hours before you leave. It's a bit like being stoned – they tell me . . . I'm not a junkie – I'm really this old.

But everyone in Los Angeles seems stoned. I don't know if they are but they seem it. It's all: 'Have a nice day . . . You're welcome.' At first I thought it was a good thing to say. Then I realised they're not listening. It just comes out blooooorghhh – like vomit. You can test them to see if they mean it. 'Have a nice day.' 'Show us your willy.' 'You're welcome.'

Even the muggers say it now. And they're all health freaks the muggers there – they eat fig seeds and jog. They have jogging muggers or juggers as they call them. Or else they're on roller skates – him and his china lift you up and beat the shit out of you.

We had this Mexican driver who was always stoned: the whole works, nose pinned to the windscreen, driving perfectly at three miles an hour. And one day he offered me one of those pills that look like submarines. And I went: 'What's *that*?' Morphine suppositories. Drugs up your jacksie? Because your nose is full, I suppose.

If you want to take morphine, fair enough, please yourself, I'll come to the funeral. Even wear a tie. But I was trying to imagine what the party would be like . . . Trying to look cool as though you've been everywhere. And everyone's passing the joint . . . sighhhhh . . . 'Heeeere.' The most used word in America: 'Here.' 'No thanks, man, I've got one of these.' Take out the suppository, shove it up your bum, whoosh. Have to walk a bit, of course – you've got to chew them. When the capsule breaks you get what's known as the bum's rush. It must be a weird feeling – you don't feel a thing but your bum's high.

We were playing at the Roxy on Sunset Strip which is a prestigious kind of place. I was opening for Ian Hunter who used to be Mott the Hoople. The audience consisted of about four hundred stoned Puerto Ricans. All holding hands trying to get in touch with the living. Living proof that there's life after death. Twelve minutes I lasted. I was supposed to be on for a week.

But it must have been terrible for them. If you're very stoned and there's a Scotsman with a banjo and banana boots trying to make you laugh . . .

One thing they do in Hollywood is put cocaine on their willy to help them keep it up. So now I always have a salt cellar of cocaine on the bedside table.

What amazes me is that all the 'What's your sign?' thing is still alive and well there. I always used to be into it, too, until it was destroyed for me when I was going out with a lovely woman who worked for the *Evening Times* in Glasgow. I was waiting for her one night and she was about five minutes late and says: 'Sorry I'm late, Bill. I finished early so they made me do the Stars.' The Stars was just something they gave whichever reporter was first finished.

Still, I love when people mispronounce the signs – Piss-case. What kind of sign is that?

They've had to introduce new ones: Pyrex – that's for test-tube babies.

I was worried that I wouldn't be understood with my accent in America but, in fact, it's not a problem although there are an awful lot of people who say 'Pardon' all the time when they know damn well what you're saying.

My Uncle Charlie's been in America for forty-seven years and he still sounds as though he's just arrived from Partick. I asked him why his accent hadn't changed at all and he said he'd never found a better one.

You get a lot of Scots who really get into the whole middle-America thing, the white shoes, the lot. Usually it's some Aberdonian guy who's got a job in Houston and he comes back talking like Gary Cooper: 'Hey, you sonofabitch.' Three weeks earlier it was: 'Whit like, mon? Aye.' and now it's instant Tex Ritter, asking for highballs in some Scottish pub where it goes down *enormously* well if you refer to the bloke behind the bar as: 'Hey, bartender!'

And there's the other kind of Scot you meet out there who's just visiting and has to complain about everything, the sort of Alastairs who tell you about jetlag and the spicy Mexican food and want to find a golfcourse. Deeply boring people.

Still, they got Andrew Carnegie about whom it was said that he gave money away as silently as a waiter falling down a flight of stairs with a tray of glasses.

1. A break by the pool in LA (as we call it).

2. This is a restaurant in Grapevine, Texas. I don't think it's for vegetarians.

3. I danced with a girl who danced with an armadillo who danced with the Prince of Wales. A charming Dallas vignette.

Miami's become very popular for British people as a place to go for holidays. God knows why. Why do they think American people never go there? Because it's wonderful? All that happens there is you get battered over the head while an alligator bites your ankles. Still, I found that the people of Miami were right behind me – I managed to throw them off at the airport. It's not a very pretty place, either. All that concrete. Why can they not have colourful cement – tartan or something?

But Reagan. An out-of-work actor gets a job as leader of the most powerful country in the world. If the Russians attack America, he'll tell the troops to form the wagons in a circle. Haig's just as bad. When Reagan was shot, Haig jumped in and wanted to play at being the President. It was like *Doctor Strangelove*.

I suppose Reagan feels OK cutting welfare payments of old people. He can go up to guys of seventy in wheelchairs, grab them by their lapels and say: 'When I was your age, I was *working*.'

When we were in the Middle East, we saw a bit in the papers about Mrs Reagan and the death penalty. She said: 'If there was a death penalty, there'd be a lot more people alive today.' What?

The gun thing in America never ceases to amaze me. The hunters are so crazy there that they have reached the stage of painting the word COW on the side of cows to let them know what not to shoot. The main gear for the hunter now is a white jacket with red, green and yellow stripes on it so that you don't get mistaken for an elk.

In Boston there was a case of a bartender who saw a man with a gun – he was an off-duty cop – and phoned the police to say that there was an armed man in his bar. So they all burst in with guns drawn. The poor off-duty cop thinks there's a raid taking place so he opens up. He kills one of them and they kill him. Bang bang.

When I was performing in Massachusetts I got to know a state trooper, a nice bloke. One time we were in café and I asked him if I could see his gun so he unloaded it, made sure all the bullets were out and handed it to me. I told my mate, Mick O'Brien, who was living in the same car park as me at the time, and he didn't believe me. So the next time I saw the trooper he was in the café with a pal, another trooper, and I asked him if he'd let Mick see the gun. So we're all four sitting round having our steaks and coffee and he unloads the gun and hands it over to Mick and by chance I looked under the table and I saw his mate had his gun out under the table pointing straight at Mick. So if he'd started any funny stuff with the gun he would have just blown him away.

I've always felt a bit funny about guns. When I was in the paratroopers I thought it would be great to be a mercenary, the whole romantic bit. Then someone shot at us in Cyprus. I can still taste the grass in my mouth. I decided I'd rather play the banjo and be a hippy than get shot at by strangers.

The latest thing they're getting into in America is how you deal with prisoners like the Ripper – they're seriously considering turning them into blood banks. Or using bits of them as spare parts.

But the creepy thing is that the Ku Klux Klan still exists and still has people joining it. They're so ridiculous those guys. I'd like to see them in a Daz commercial . . . 'Ah always do mah husband's sheets in Daz . . . gets rid of the bloodstains.' I told someone I was a wizard between the sheets and they thought I was in the Ku Klux Klan.

One thing I liked that Dick Gregory did, which Muhammad Ali then did when he was giving a lecture to students at Harvard. He says: 'How tolerant would you all be if I told you this was just burnt cork?'

Texas is one of my favourite places because it's the one place in the world where I can be short. I said that to someone in Los Angeles and they thought I said: 'It's the one place in the world where I can be shot.' They thought: The man's mad – he wants to be shot in Dallas like John Kennedy . . . In fact, we went to the place where he was shot and you get an eerie feeling as you drive past it.

A Scottish farmer was showing a Texan farmer round his wee place in Galloway. And the Texan asks: 'How big is this farm?' 'Oh – just over eight acres.' 'Walll – I have a farm in Texas and I can drive for two days and still be inside my property.' 'Aye . . . I used tae have a car like that.'

But Texas is really a different country from the rest of America. They think Margaret Thatcher is great, so you have to watch what you say a wee bit. All those blokes with guns. I get as nervous as a long-tailed cat in a roomful of rocking-chairs.

One of the characters we met in Dallas was the Texas Kid, a black cowboy who drove around in a Cadillac with bull-horns on the front. He was a seventh son and his wife was his seventh wife and she was the best – you felt a bit sorry for the other six he'd had to get through to get there. Any time he had to do something important it always had to be on the seventh of the fourteenth or the twenty-first. And he made sculptures out of whatever he found lying around: 'Nature made it, Ah just added to it.' Instead of having a deer's head mounted on his wall, he had a deer's arse. And in his garden he had found a tree trunk that looked like a pair of legs so he put a pair of shorts on them.

I was watching a cop in Dallas with a wee paper cup in his hand and I thought: That's nice, he's able to have a cup of coffee on the beat. Then he spat into it! He was chewing tobacco and what they do is carry a wee Dixie cup around with them so that they can spit into it. Most bizarre. They even have them in boardrooms I was told – you have all these American executives spitting into wee paper cups.

We went to the Will Rogers Memorial Hall for the Grand Old Oprey in Fort Worth. It was very strange. They have hosts making announcements to the audience: 'We'd like to wish a very happy birthday to Wilbur Mackenzie who's eighty-two years young tonight . . . his two daughters, Cindy and Connie, have brought him here tonight.' And everyone claps everyone else. 'A big hello to Janie Hawks who was in a head-on collision in Grapevine last week. We'd like to play "Broken Woman" for her later on – only kiddin' Jane! . . . And the members of the Wicked Widow Society who have asked Joyce to sing "One Day at a Time" . . . and I've had a request for all the people with hats on to take them off because the short people can't see. In a minute Wanda is going to sing "Love Is Fair – It Breaks Everybody's Heart" for Elmer and Shirley Harris whose fortieth anniversary it is tonight . . . I don't think we can get the spotlight onto them but we know they're there somewhere.'

Quite extraordinary. And they had a harmonica player who could stand on his hands, the runner-up in the Miss Texas pageant and a country and western ventriloquist. And then they brought on Wanda Jackson who did this: 'Well, ladies and gentlemen, I'd like to tell you about a very special day in my life: 7 June 1971 . . . Because until that day it looked as though I had everything – a husband, two children, good health, a successful career, influential friends – but despite it all I was empty inside. And that's when I invited Jesus into my life . . .' – It was all like that.

When I was in Nashville I was in a bar talking to a woman who had a very bad speech impediment and she asked me if I would like her to sing a song for me. So I said, 'Sure', and she got up on the stage and sang that Johnny Ray classic 'Cry' and it was fantastic. She was all drunk but she had a lovely singing voice. There are some wonderful singers there, though two of my favourite American singers, John Prine and Steve Goodman, aren't from there at all.

Grapevine is another Texas town we went to and the Oprey there had a comic on telling jokes about Aggies who are apparently these local idiots, agricultural students, but the jokes are exactly the same as you hear told about the Irish by bad English comedians or about the Polish in America so it wasn't exactly a rib-tickling night.

However, they have a place called Aquarina Springs or something where they have pigs swimming underwater. It's apparently quite amazing. They put on a whole show underwater with a couple having a picnic underwater which you watch through this screen – they drink a bottle of lemonade which is apprently difficult to do underwater – and then a pig swims by. Sounds quite unreal . . . and I had always thought that pigs couldn't swim.

In Texas they also have a discotheque with sharks swimming round in a pool as you dance. We hope to open one in Scotland with tadpoles in it. Everything certainly is bigger there – the Amfac hotel where we stayed in Dallas was so big that the lazier people got driven around it in a sort of caddy car thing.

The cowboy thing is still very strong there – I'd love to do a film where every line was one of those clichés: 'Apaches? This far south? . . . They never attack at night . . .' Whoosh! 'An arrow? Where's Jake? In the chuck waggon . . .'

One thing I love in America is the car stickers. You see battered old Volkswagens with 'My Other Car Is a Porsche'. And in California you get 'Have You Hugged your Cat Today?' What an idea! Probably make you vomit. In Texas there was one that said 'Have You Hugged your Horse Today?'

And I like those places in America that give themselves honest names: in LA there was a place called the Fatburger and a shop called Trashy Lingerie. And a carwash place that said 'Satisfaction guaranteed or your dirt back'. And a Jewish chicken place we saw there as well called the Kosher Kolonel.

Americans can certainly eat. I've never seen such enormous helpings – and such enormous people in my life. The size of some of their bums! They're like polythene bags full of bellybuttons . . . they walk in the sand and leave no footsteps behind them – they wipe out all trace with their bums, they're that close to the ground.

In Dallas we found this shop called Nieman Marcus – well possibly someone had found it before us – which is the Harrods of Texas. On the way out they were doing some survey so we had to fill in a questionnaire. They had a box for you to tick if you had had higher education, a degree, a postgraduate degree and so on. So I couldn't tick off any of them. Then they had one for how much you earned and I ticked the More Than $100,000 box so I hope they looked at it and thought: How come this uneducated bastard is earning so much?

Nieman Marcus were selling this Age-Controlling Creme when we were in there so I thought, why not? and bought a jar. And Nick Roeg was there and said he was the only one who realised that I wasn't buying it as a joke.

They had what I never thought I'd live to see which was cowboy boots with studs in them so that you can play golf in them. The golfing cowboy, I ask you . . . But we found out why they have their cowboy hats turned up at the sides: it's so that three of them can get into a pickup truck together with their hats on. And they have them with all feathers at the front – I rather fancy one with a whole pheasant on it.

But the puzzling thing about shopping in LA is that you can't find the simplest things. I went in to get some milk – not the most devastatingly difficult task you would think – milk. In a bottle. Computes easily. But not in Los Angeles. They had thirty-seven different kinds, one of which was guaranteed to contain no dairy product . . . Where do they get it from? Bloody monkeys?

What really puzzles me though is those wee containers of milk you get with your coffee in America – how on earth do the cows get it into such a small container?

We went to the Comedy Store in Los Angeles and there were some very funny blokes there but they have that thing of using the word 'fuck' too much. Lenny Bruce was very good on that; he used to go 'fuck, fuck, fuck, fuck, fuck,' just to make the word meaningless. But some comedians use it all the time which is silly because it is the most powerful of swear words and it destroys its power if you use it all the time. But I liked some of the lines: 'Can I borrow a cigarette – I left mine in the machine . . . Ah, you remind me very much of myself when your age . . . foreign aid is when the poor people of a rich country have their money given to the rich people of a poor country.' But a lot of their stuff is that: 'I just got rid of a hundred pounds of unsightly flesh – divorced my wife,' which is exactly the same sort of stuff as you can get anywhere. And some of these New Wave comedians in Britain are getting into a kind of Singalongalternativecomedy sort of style.

In Hollywood, too, there's a guy who makes a living – this is true – by plucking the grey hairs off male go-go dancers. He would have been a hit on 'What's My Line', wouldn't he? Aye, you can tell when you're in Hollywood – weird things like that and nearly whole cigarettes left in the ashtrays.

I saw Charles Manson being interviewed by a guy on the telly in LA and he was saying that he had done his time, that he was harmless and that he should be let out but that people didn't want him out of jail 'Because they're frightened I'll break their toys . . .' Woooooooooo . . .

Heard this joke in Hollywood: there are three dogs. Each represents a profession. One is the mathematician's dog; one is the architect's and one the record company executive's. And in this room are three piles of biscuits. So . . . the mathematician's dog comes up to the first pile, takes two biscuits and three biscuits, makes an equals sign with another two biscuits and then puts down five biscuits. And the other dogs go, 'Aye, very good.' Then the architect's dog takes the second pile and very carefully constructs this perfect geodesic dome with the biscuits. And the other dogs go, 'Very nice, aye.' Then the record company executive's dog comes along, fucks the other two dogs, crunches the biscuits, snorts then, and takes the rest of the afternoon off.

In America I also discovered this new drink called a Zombie which is very popular in LA for obvious reasons. It's a Polynesian thing and you get it in a half coconut. It looks like chocolate milk, there's things in it, lumps, and it's a bit sweet. It's the strangest thing in the world because you get drunk from the feet up. Your head's sober and you're chatting away and you've had four of them and your face is all chocolate milk. Then you have to go to the toilet and you get up and WHAM! Out.

Marty Feldman plays in one of those Sunday football teams out there, all the expatriates, but they always complain about him because he's hell to play against – you can't tell from looking him in the eyes which way he's about to go.

When I was on the tour with Elton John I *nearly* saw Elvis. He came to one of the concerts but he was so surrounded by his minders that I didn't even get to see his trouser-leg. I'm not a star in the States by any manner of means. If you've got sun and open-topped cars you don't have much need for Scottish comedians with banjos, do you?

The Elton tour was odd: I was playing before he came on in Washington and I got hit on the head by a pipe that someone threw. And at that very moment my daughter Cara woke up screaming in Drymen. Ahhhhh . . . Kids are meant to be a great comfort in your old age but I think they play a large part in speeding up the process. It's funny with Cara – I phoned up from LA to speak to my wife and, with the phone costing about a hundred dollars a minute, Cara's telling me about her sausage sizzle with the Brownies and then she goes: 'Ma – it's Billy Connolly.'

Elton goes down amazingly well but I saw the Sex Pistols doing their number in a Texas bar, some sort of Longhorn Bar with all the guys in stetsons and they were looking at these weird English guys – Sid Vicious had that strange colour to his face that people who take drugs get, like alabaster, he looked like something out of Madame Tussaud's – and the cowboys started throwing cans of Lone Star beer at them and the cans just bounce off them . . . Boing, Boing . . . and the band goes right on playing. Then Sid Vicious goes: 'You want to hurt us? This is how you do it,' and he started bashing his face with his guitar. There's blood streaming down his face and he's spitting it out at the cowboys. They didn't know *where* to look. They're all looking at each other and wondering, Ho, hum, maybe we should go back and pick up the gun. The lovely thing about Sid Vicious was that he did that version of 'My Way', walking down a flight of steps and giving V-signs. And the great thing about it was that of all the thousands of people who have sung 'My Way', Sid was the only one who *really* did it his way. Anyway, I think all the Sex Pistols were great.

Down there in the cowboy country there's a whole chain of restaurants called Roy Rogers Restaurants. I used to go in and ask for a Triggerburger. It didn't go down well. Instant diarrhoea – it gives 'happy trails to you' a whole new meaning. His dog was called Bullet – that's what I looked like heading for the toilet. Actually, it was called Rebel, wasn't it? Or was that Champion the Wonder Horse's pal? I don't know – I need treatment. I keep veering off.

The Scottish-Americans like to tell you that if you want to identify tartans it's easy – you look under the kilt and if it's a quarter-pounder, it's a McDonald's. They're more to be pitied than scolded.

Another restaurant we bumped into in LA was a Chinese place called The Yangtse Doodle – only in America.

But what you notice more than the food out there is the drugs. Everyone in California is permanently stoned.

Keith Moon was having a party in LA once and they heard that the police were going to come round and raid it. So everyone clears all the dope out of sight and the cop comes in – jodhpurs, boots, hat, the lot – a motorcycle cop. Walks round the whole house looking under the cushions and in the drawers but he finds nothing. All the guests are sitting around biting their tongues. Then he sees a wee bottle on the mantelpiece. Oh-ho. Goes over and sniffs it. And it's amyl nitrate – which (I am told) has an immediate effect of hilarity on the taker. So the poor man staggers off giggling hysterically onto his motorbike and back into the night.

Most of the coke dealers there are mixing the cocaine up with talcum powder. People are tooting it and getting overwhelmed with the desire to move to Florida and dye their hair blue.

The police there are funny, too. The ones in San Diego I was hearing about, decided (commendably enough) to try and break down the barriers between them and the public. So they put pink pig transfers on the side of their squad cars! They also had to take off their hats so they wouldn't look so threatening – there's nothing worse than a bloke in a peaked cap coming and knocking on your front door.

Another thing they did was to allow anyone who wanted to ride in the squad car with them to do so, if they would agree to sign a wee bit of paper saying they wouldn't sue the police if they got their head blown off. And apparently most of the squad cars leaving the stations are full now – old age pensioners who find it a damn sight more entertaining than washing their pyjamas and young girls who like the Starsky and Hutch number. I'm not sure if it would work in Britain – too much of your time you'd be seeing to an alarm that had gone off in a shoeshop . . . but something needs to be done here because the whole barrel is falling over.

But at least we haven't reached that stage they have in New York where they need special vigilantes in the subway. I have my own method of getting a bit of elbow room when travelling on the subway: I take an egg with me, surreptitiously break it open into a hankie, then do one of those exaggerated sneezes that bring lots of snotters out – then you hold the hankie away from your face and you've got all this yellow gooey stuff dribbling down your hands. There's not many people want to come close to you after that.

Oscars are something I wouldn't mind winning at all . . . I liked it when *Reds* won the best director award and they were playing 'The Internationale' as Warren Beatty went up to get his Oscar. There were all the punters in the audience in the bow-ties and the organdie dresses with the music that you associate with scarves and bonnets . . . and you think of that line in it: 'Away with cant . . .'

But there do seem to be an awful lot of awards, someone's winning something every week – which is why we had that 'Other Awards' ceremony after all the BAFTA ones because it was all getting a bit too serious. . . . 'Best All-round Entertainer Whose Name begins with P and Who Comes from Within Fifty Miles Radius of Corby'. And at some of the award ceremonies they try and find out whether you could be there to receive your wee prize, and if you can't make it because you're working in Cornwall, then you don't get the prize – because they hate some stranger getting up from beside his pals and going to get the award 'on behalf' of someone . . .

Steve Martin, the American comedian, does a lovely routine of an Oscar-winner: his name is announced, he does all that looking-flushed bit and kissing his friends and shaking people's hands as he walks along the row, down the aisle and then onto the stage, gets the wee gold man and says 'I don't need to thank *anybody*! I DID IT MYSELF. IT WAS ME, ME, ME! NO-ONE HELPED ME! I WAS OUT THERE ON MY OWN . . .' I'm sure some of the winners would love to do that.

Not that I'm holding my breath about picking up Oscars – my one major movie experience to date is lying in a grave after being killed by some bloke in *Absolution*. The guy who kills me is the actor who played Kes in that film – there, that's ruined the plot for anyone who hasn't seen it. Richard Burton played the priest in the film and he comes into the forest and finds my body there, in the shallow grave (they always have to be shallow graves for some reason). He has to do this dead serious scene of seeing the body and realising that I've been murdered by one of his pupils, very emotional moment. So I'm lying there with all the leaves and earth and things in my face as he's about to start and so I sang 'I belong to Glasgow'. He was very nice about it. I would have hit him with a spade if he'd done that to me.

Americans take their films very seriously and their TV ratings – same as in Britain, I suppose, you have to get a good rating or it's not a good programme. Which is daft. Hitler got a good audience – does that mean he was good?

Though one film I was in – *The Secret Policeman's Other Ball* – there's a lovely bit when Donovan comes on to sing. One of the audience says: 'I thought you were dead!' Donovan says: 'Not yet'.

The American movies I used to like were those with a dock scene where Marlon Brando's in a vest and everyone crowds round the dock gates hoping that they'll get thrown the tag and get work . . . which is actually what used to happen on the Clyde as well. And when you read about all the shortage of work here and the papers closing down you think about owners of newspapers coming out of the front doors on Fleet Street with six typewriters under their arm and throwing them out to all the hungry reporters.

I hope that whole McCarthy thing doesn't come back to Hollywood again. Not that McCarthy was much more than a loonie – he used to appear in one American town in the morning and say he'd got a list of 424 known communist subversives. Then he'd fly off to the next town and by then he'd have lost the place and he would say he had 279. By the end of the day it would be four. A lot of it was obviously just made up as he went along and the sad thing is that so many people in Hollywood went along with it.

They'd have a fit in America if they had the rail unions refusing to handle a newspaper – I like the British Rail unions did with the *Sun* after the *Sun* had accused them of spending their time in boozers and discos. I thought it was great that the unions wouldn't touch the paper – I thought 'Now you're whistling, Dixie.'

I love going to America and being away. As Dan Hicks says in his song – 'How can I miss you if you won't go away?'

EUROVISION
SONG CONTEST
FRANCE
BELGIUM
NETHERLANDS
GERMANY
SPAIN
NORWAY
GREECE
JUGOSLAVIA
UNITED KINGDOM
LUXEMBOURG
JIBROVIA
FINLAND
EASY!!
EASY!!!
JIBROVIA

EUROPE

The scene is the Cannes Film Festival: a middle-aged producer, the belly over the trousers, the medallion in the chest hair, the Porsche sunglasses . . . comes up to this young starlet . . .

'Hello . . . I've been watching you for the last two days and – I know it must sound corny, particularly here – but I love the way you move. It's so . . . eloquent. And I like your voice . . . Yes, I've been listening to the way you talk to people, the way you project yourself. And, well . . . it's perfect for – I might as well tell you, no point in beating about the bush: I have this property in my pocket – a script. We hope to start on location at the end of the year and . . . well, I know I'm biased but I think it could be great, really great. And it could be a great vehicle for you to make a real name for yourself, to really achieve something of *significance*. Not just commercially – although of course our backers have to consider that – but artistically as well. I'd love to talk to you more about it because, as I say, I think you are the very person that I had been hoping for – not with any great expectation of success I might say because such presence is so rare – to complete the jigsaw puzzle. Because, without wanting to boast or anything this is going to be some production. So much has already been set up, so much talent is already committed to it . . . We've got Coppola directing of course . . .'

'Oh, wow!' she says, 'Francis Ford Coppola!'

'No – Reg Coppola. A wonderful, wonderful director . . . and the male lead is – Redford.'

'Robert Redford!'

'No, *Brian* Redford. A fine, fine actor. The music is being arranged by Previn . . .'

'André Previn?'

'No – Alistair Previn. And the dance routines will be arranged by Blair?'

'Lionel Blair . . .?'

'That's right.'

I did a Burns Night in Paris. It was one of those societies called St Andrew's or Waverley or something like that. They've all got different names over there, like the Daughters of Caledonia who are a bit of a scruffy mob, not like the Daughters of the American Revolution who see themselves as being middle-classish; this lot is a bit down-marketish, more like the Eastern Cross. Some of them are really nice people and I can quite see why they join – though I wouldn't – in those foreign circumstances.

But what I found most confusing was in New Jersey, in a place called Kearney, which had a Scottish club. A friend of mine, Sammy McEwan, a Celtic supporter, was a barman there. And while I was having a wee chat with him this guy in a green blazer comes in, it's one of those blazers with a shamrock on the pocket – I don't know why I say one of those blazers with a shamrock because I've never seen one like it before or since but anyway . . . 'What are ye daein' here?' he asks. 'Well . . . this is the Scottish club and I'm – ' 'Och, ye're a Celtic supporter – you should be at the Irish club.'

So it gets all confusing: Scots guys who support Celtic go to the Irish club; Scots guys who support Rangers go to the Scottish club; Irish guys who couldn't care less go to the Irish club; Scottish guys who are fanatical Rangers supporters go to the *Ulster* club. They all take their wee bigotries with them in their luggage.

Still, I suppose if you're in Medicine Hat or Edmonton or some-where it's nice to walk into those clubs and talk about Celtic or Motherwell or Thistle because you miss the nitty gritty of where you come from. For me it sucks a bit – but that's not fair because I just walk in and out again.

Back to Paris, though. It was quite an upmarket do – accountants and lawyers. And they are well into the Scottish culture so I had to do my homework very heavily because I was doing The Immortal Memory which is the main speech. There was a boy from Stirling who had obviously been to a few stag nights in Scotland and thought that was the way to do it – he was doing the Toast to the Lassies. The punters were furious with his jokes – shouting at him and telling him to sit down and they weren't even pissed.

But the do was bloody splendid. The thing I liked about it was that it wasn't all Moss Bros kilts – these guys had had their kilts for years. And they had sparklers in the haggis! I knew Burns was guilty of many things but blowing up the Houses of Parliament wasn't one of them.

My whole theme was that Burns was alive and well in such a strange way. They push him like a rock singer. I had albums and calendars and magazines and posters and place mats, postcards, all the bumph and paraphernalia and even those copies of his letters and poems which are done as if they were on parchment, that burnt effect.

There was a Presbyterian minister there – they have a big Church of Scotland in Paris – and he was openly hostile to my coming to the gig but a few fans had pushed it through. So I was quoting 'Holy Willie's Prayer' and Burns' attitude to the Presbyterian Church, which he was by no means enamoured of. He was all for Jacobites. And his material is alive and well – what else was the Ayatollah doing in Paris but nursing his wrath to keep it warm?

In Scotland the Burns experts often know the one poem and that's them: a Burns Man. The Brylcreem hair and the wee moustache, trying to look like a mason. What they don't realise is that when Burns was a freemason, it was a radical society, very very anti-landlord, rebellious. And they have now become what the original ones were fighting.

It was all in the Excelsior in Paris – it was to have been in the George V but they needed a bigger place. It ended up in total decadence. The person you arrived with bore no resemblance to the person you left with. Everyone was fighting for the microphone by the end, pissed and singing songs from the stage. The pianist had a lady up his kilt.

In Amsterdam, demonstrators put down lions' shit, which they get from the zoo, on the streets, and it scares the police horses. Works a treat apparently.

There's a whole generation of people whose only knowledge of tigers is through circuses and they've grown up believing that a tiger is frightened of a chair. 'If you ever go in the jungle, make sure you take a chair with you.' Same thing with big tops – when wee boys see them in Scotland they say: 'Christ – look at the size o' that tent! I'd like tae see the rucksack.'

One thing I do find hard to get used to on the Continent is the beer: Heineken reaches parts other beers don't – right behind the eyeballs.

In Denmark I met up with a band that had one bloke in it called Hans Nilson and another called Nils Hansen and I wanted them to call themselves 'Hans, Nils and Boomsadaisy' but apparently when it was translated into Danish it wasn't quite so hilarious.

I was with them one time – and with another Glasgow bloke – when a fight broke out in the bar and there was glass and blood everywhere. And Nils was teasing us and saying: 'What about the great Glasgow hardmen? You two were the first out of the bar when the fighting started.' But we each had our drinks still in our hands – everybody else was out on the street by now but their drinks were still inside.

A honeymoon couple are lying in their bed in the hotel off St Mark's Square in Venice. They've just made love – there's that trace of sweat in the air – and they're feeling great. 'Oh . . . darling . . . that was wonderful, really wonderful.' 'Mmmmm . . . it was soooo gooood, wasn't it?' 'Mmmmm.' The sun comes up slowly and outside in the distance they can just hear the strains of a mandolin. 'What's that tune he's playing, darling?' she asks. 'It's a selection from the *Gondoliers*.' 'How funny – that's what the doctor said I had.'

My definition of an intellectual is someone who can listen to the *William Tell Overture* without thinking of the Lone Ranger.

The only thing I can remember about being in Germany was for some strange reason looking in the telephone directory to see if there was anyone called Adolf Hitler. And there wasn't.

Another Handy Fact from the Continent is that John Philip Sousa's real name wasn't Sousa. It was So. (No, it wasn't! It was *So*! No, it wasn't . . .) Still, as they said on 'Swap Shop', Keep Britain Tidy – send your rubbish to France.

It's odd being in countries that Britain was once at war with and you're brought up thinking of them as baddies. It's like my lucky uncle Freddy (who, you may remember, got shot in the First World War by a German bullet that bounced off his gold watch that covered his heart and went straight up his left nostril and blew his head off) . . . well, when he went off to fight he told his mother

'There's a war going on and I'm off to fight.' And his mother said 'Oh, aye – who are the baddies?' 'I don't know – but some guy in the pub told me they were a bunch of bastards.'

When I was in Holland with the Humblebums, I met a soldier and his wife and they were on holiday from Berlin. He was on Checkpoint Charlie. Neither of them were the Brain of Britain and his wife was saying: 'Our John has to go out and guard that wall from thae communists.' And I asked her if she'd ever seen a communist. 'Oh, no . . .' She was talking about them like they were dinosaurs. So I said 'D'you have any idea what they're like?' 'Aye – I saw them on television and they've all got big long coats.' And I thought Jesus Christ, this person thinks her husband goes out in the morning and defends the world from men in big, long coats, stops them from eating people's children . . .

And a variation on that, a story that a bloke called Hector tells, has this Scottish bloke, nice, polite, friendly fellow, having his holiday in Torremolinos. And he's talking to someone who's been there for some while and knows the ropes:
    'Em . . . every evening I hear people saying "Buenas Noches" and smiling to each other. What does it mean, do you know?'
    'Aye. It means "Good night" in Spanish and it's a sort of friendly thing to say to people.'
    'Oh, fine.'
So the next evening he's had his risotto and his salad and his bottle of vino and he's walking down the main street of Torremolinos back to the little hotel where he's staying. He sees a bunch of blokes on the far side of the street. So he thinks, right I can try that new thing I learnt:
    'Buenas Noches!'
    'Fuck off, ya Spanish bastard.'

When uncle Freddy went off they would march along 'Left, right, left, right', which was a completely new breakthrough which came about in the First World War. The Army Intelligence had spent years working on this plan for propelling men all in the same direction at the one time. Previous to that, they had had all sorts of exotic ways, like 'left, left, right, right, right, left.' And the whole thing had got a bit scattered. Freddy knew this because he remembered his uncle Willy who'd fought in the Boer War; he had had a

94

really peculiar way of marching which was 'left, left, left, left, left' which made him a very easy target for snipers because he was going round and round in the same direction.

The other thing they would have on the Western Front were regimental mascots, little Scottie dogs. Which are greatly to be preferred to those funny miniature creatures that you see yapping around the streets in Chelsea. Though I dare say I would yap around and be angry if my balls dragged along the pavement all the time.

A friend of mine, Brian Wilson, interviewed Lev Yashin, the Russian goalie, when he was in Moscow . . . Yashin was this great hero and had become a manager or a coach. And they were talking about the Rangers fans who went wild in Barcelona during the final of the Cupwinners' Cup there and Yashin had been there at the time. He didn't speak English but through his interpreter Brian was getting words like 'scandalasky' coming out because he had been amazed at their behaviour, never seen anything like it, tra-la-la. So Brian told him that it was reported that it was the first defeat that the fascist police in Spain had suffered and Yashin fell about the floor laughing, never having thought of it in that way.

When I was in Copenhagen with some friends who'd been performing over there – I was hanging around on a street corner wearing the lot – the clogs, denim suit, earrings, long hair – chatting to a bunch of Danish friends. And Celtic were playing a European Cup match over there so the supporters were out in force. And a wee bloke came down, sort of leading his pals along. He was dressed in that way: the V-neck sweater with no shirt underneath, the bell-bottom jeans, high-heeled boots, tattoo on the arm with 'Bonnie Scotland' on it, the green and white scarf. And he saw us hanging out there, obviously thought we were a bunch of Danish hippies, so he looks at us and goes 'Ya *wankers*'. And I looked at him and said 'Who are ye calling a wanker – ya bampot!' The Scots are so sweet to each other abroad.

PRINCIPAL EXPORTS —

	DOGS
	RUBBER WEAR
	SHIRTS
	BLACK PUDDINGS
	HAEMORRHOIDS
	PUBLIC SCHOOLBOYS

Wetwang

Birmingham

London

ENGLAND

hen I travelled with Danny Kyle on the folkie scene we used to go by train a lot. One trick we had was to go into the toilet with stink bombs, those wee round ones. Now on the bottom of the lavatory seats are four wee black rubber knobs. What we would do is put the stink bomb on one of those, tape it on with black tape so it couldn't be seen, then hang around outside. The first person to go in would put the seat down and there would be this most disgusting smell. Then we would bang on the door and go: 'Hurry up, in there . . . JESUS! What a smell.' And the poor bloke would be inside, unable to open the window yet not wanting to come out – he'd be stuck in there all the way to London . . .

Another one is the film across the lavatory seat – that transparent stuff you wrap food in. So you go in for a crap and the shit goes all over your trousers – or you have a piss and it bounces off.

One time I was driving around London with Ralph McTell and we got completely lost. And suddenly I thought – wait a minute, this is the man who wrote 'Let me take you by the hand, I'll lead you through the streets of London' – this is the great authority on the subject and he doesn't know where the hell we are.

When I was staying in Fulham, I liked going into the pubs round there. They're dead friendly although I think there's some brewers' agreement that there has to be one wanker in every pub. Without fail, there's always one.

What you don't get which I did a bit of in Scotland was the guy who comes and calls you a prick . . . 'Aye, I know you – you steal all your patter frae pubs . . .'

I was in this pub in Fulham and there was a regular there, a bloke with a withered arm. And his mates persuaded him to try a game of darts. So he tucks the darts in his top pocket because he can't hold them in his other hand. Throws the first. Throws the second. Then he throws his pen! Everyone roars with laughter and so does he.

And I was sitting in there having a pint and listening to that song, the romantic one the Fureys sing 'When you're Sweet Sixteen' – and I said: 'Aye, if my faither was here he'd be greetin'.' And this old bloke sitting next to me at the bar goes: 'And if my father was here, it'd be a bloody miracle.'

Another bloke in there works in the antique trade which was a bit of an eye-opener because he would come in and say: 'I'm knackered – I've just made a sixteenth-century picture frame.'

And just round the corner was Dan Leno Walk. Apparently Dan Leno was given a golden tiepin by King George V as a token of his esteem. And Leno gave it away to a barmaid, which is nice.

Elton John played at the Palace and before he started the Queen Mother said to him: 'You may hear a noise during the middle of this – a loud noise followed by a dragging sound. That'll be someone falling off his chair and being dragged away. Don't let it put you off . . .'

And Elton's manager John Reed was with him and was dancing with the Queen Mother and she said: 'Oh, you must meet a lot of interesting people in your job . . .'

Poor Charles. Why does he keep falling off his horse? I thought they were going to put safety belts in the royal carriage at his wedding. And he's going bald too. I told him to get a transplant but he thought he'd look silly with a kidney on the top of his head.

Still, I was delighted when Di got pregnant – it got me out of the news sharpish. I meant to write and thank them – Jimmy Tarbuck's got the address.

Those wedding presents they got were amazing – hundreds and hundreds of them. But as Lady Di said to Angela Rippon, with a tear in either eye: 'We have two houses to fill.'

One thing I do envy the royals is their wee chins: shaving must be a doddle – whoosh, and it's all done in one stroke.

Still there is that lovely photo of the Queen and Lady Di standing together. Di's so much taller – she looks as though she's working her.

What amazes me, though, is the House of Lords and the fact that there are people like Jennie Lee in it, people who've rubbished privilege all their lives and then they want some. Look at Shirley Williams and all the stuff she comes up with about how undemocratic the block vote was – yet she was kept on the executive all these years by the block vote.

I liked that McAllister cartoon in the *Guardian* about the time of the Crosby by-election that said: 'The only people who aren't voting for Shirley Williams are the people who've moved here from her last constituency.'
    She's awfully good at that 'I am concerned' look. And the Busy Look, with the folder under the arm.

How do you tell when a politician is lying? You can see their lips moving.

But the SDP are a funny lot. I think they're the kind of people who offer you just one digestive biscuit with your tea. They live in the kind of houses where the ashtrays don't have adverts on them. And I'm sure they'll start elbowing out all the Liberal candidates – they don't want all those walking-stick salesmen, do they?

The Tories are easier to spot at a distance: they're the ones with the tufts on their cheeks . . . And they keep hunting for Trotskyists everywhere. Yet when you ask them what a Trotskyist is, they don't know. Them and spies they like to get after: I felt sorry for all those old boys who were dragged out as traitors. That Leo Long came over as a nice honest man to me because he said that the Russians seemed to be more anti-fascist than we were at the time, which seems fair enough.

I was in Brighton for one of the Tory conferences – always an odd experience, all those drunks wandering round the street. You keep seeing cabinet ministers and so on. And have you ever seen such a soapy soutar as Denis Thatcher?

Still, I like what he said when someone asked him how he slept at night: 'I sleep like a baby – I wake up every two hours crying and wetting myself.'

Lots of foreigners who come to England see Hyde Park and everyone talking there and assume because of that that we have free speech. Not true.

And the other wrong idea they get is that the average British worker is a lazy sod. Which again is not true – (I love crawling to the readers – my knees are all blood).

And when the *West Highland Free Press* was new they did a big union piece in support of trade unions, which I completely agreed with. But for a joke I wrote a spoof letter to them, haranguing them for their attitude to those terrible creatures who brought the nation to its knees and held the country to ransom. And I signed it: 'William J. Connolly, in the hope of a swift return of Oswald Mosley' – he was still alive then. I thought it was a laugh.

Then I met the boys, Brian and the lads from the *Free Press*. and told them that I'd sent a letter but they'd never acknowledged it. But they had thought it was *serious* – they couldn't read the signature but had noticed that the street the bloke wrote from was the same as mine and they were going to warn me that some right-wing loonie was living near me and that I should watch out for him . . .

I once saw a film of Mosley at Olympia or somewhere like that. It was like Nuremburg. It was extraordinary and I remember the commentator saying that the uproar on that occasion was not so much because of his politics but because of his bouncers – he had about one bouncer for every three people, a real aggro-incitement industry he had going.

It's odd that people don't draw more parallels between what he was up to and what the National Front have been trying to do, the whole fascist number, but the connection doesn't get made all that often – they link them with the neo-fascists on the Continent but they don't recall so often that Mosley was up to the same tricks fifty years ago. It was amazing the way Mosley was rehabilitated after he died – all those newspapers writing about him like he was some distinguished elder statesman instead of a fascist loonie.

His nephew was in the parachute regiment with me. Max Mosley – he had red hair but he looked like that skeletal figure that Giles draws, Chalky the schoolteacher, and he had all Hooray-Henry friends similar to himself. At that time Mosley was in the news a lot because there were race riots going on. So in the paras whenever they did the roll-call and called out 'Mosley' everyone would hoot with laughter.

But I heard a story about the first Lancaster bomber that was delivered to the airforce. They took it out to test it over Filingdale Moor in Yorkshire. And the bomb-aimer goes: 'Three degrees starboard, Number One . . . ZZZZZ . . . One degree port . . . ZZ . . . Down a hundred feet . . . WOOOOMMM . . . Open the bomb doors.' So they did. And the night shift fell out.

The press likes to foster these ideas, though. And the ones I can't stand are the ones who tell you that their politics are left even though they work for the *Daily Express*. Why don't they just own up?

Gossip columnists are the worst. They're all Jessies, that 'Did you know that? . . . Oooo . . . well I never!' stuff. All that energy to find out if someone went out with someone else. They're that magic breed of men who sit on top of your roof with a telephoto lens and then accuse you of being a publicity-seeker. The most constructive thing they could do is file down the top of their camera so that it's easier to shove it up their arse. I had one who told my manager the room number of the hotel I'd been in in Morocco – who needs the KGB when you've got that lot around? They say their readers want to know who's sleeping with whom but I think it's really *them* that wants to know.

But it's worse for the people who had no intention at all of being in the public eye. Those reporters who go round to someone's house when the son's been killed on a motorbike and they ask the mother what she thinks of motorbikes now. What do they think she thinks of motorbikes – that they're warm and cuddly? All this shit about 'I'm only doing my job'. It's no excuse.

Some people seem to get away with it. Jess Yates got done for going off with another woman, but Bruce Forsyth didn't. It seems to go in turns. I was at a reception and a friend handed one of the gossip writers a wee note and asked him to give it to me – and the note said: 'I'm only a creepy gossip columnist but I'd like to fuck you.'

Frank Zappa said about rock journalism that it was people who can't write, interviewing people who can't speak for people who can't read.

And so often they get it wrong, too. I was once doing an interview about Scots who'd gone off the rails through the booze and I was talking about the boxer, Benny Lynch. When it appeared, it had become *Kenny* Lynch. Fortunately he has a sense of humour and thought it was hilarious, and was cracking jokes about being in the Black Watch.

The critics I like are the ones who write a review for a show they haven't seen – then the show is cancelled without them knowing and the review still goes in the paper. There used to be a football writer for a Scottish paper who would just sit in the pub and wait for the punters to come in after the game and he'd just get a consensus of what the game was like from them and write his report from that, which is a nice enough idea.

Like most show-offs, I'm shy, which people don't believe. And often they come up if you're sitting somewhere and take pictures of you as though you were a polar bear. Some press photographers are like that, too. And they try to get pictures of you drinking – like Yootha Joyce, who was a wonderful lady and very funny. I think it was disgusting the way people went on about her boozing.

There's not many magazines I read regularly – I like bits of *Private Eye* but I don't like the way they keep going on about Jews and gays, but I suppose that's something to do with them all being public-school boys.

And a lot of the music press which I loved in the seventies seems to have gone off. They're like footballers who get old and start clogging. When they can't match the young guys, they trip them. And I think the music press is a bit like that. The fashions change so fast they can't keep up.

Travelling round England you stay at some very strange hotels. I got propositioned once at the Carlton Tower. It was very funny. I was just going out for the evening and this woman knocks on the door. 'Oh, sorry, I must have got the wrong room.' 'Aye, I'm just off.' 'Oh

. . . where are you off to?' ' Just away to have some fun.' 'Well, we could have fun right here.' So I said Cheerio. But I don't get propositioned much. I think it happens more to the smoothie types like Tom Jones and Des O'Connor. I get more men coming round to see me, telling those old jokes I last heard at school . . . Ah, Des O'Connor – listening to him is like washing a hankie.

There's one hotel in Glasgow though where if you ask for an extra pillow they send a woman up to your room. Poor Jamie my roadie just wanted an extra pillow one night and there was this wee knock on his door . . .

One of the favourite places was the Fowey hotel in St Austell. On the tour you're given this handy wee itinerary which tells you about the facilities in each place: 'twenty-four-hour service . . . tra-la-la . . . and so on'. And the Fowey hotel became legendary before we even reached it because it just said: 'A casserole will be provided.' In fact they produced – because we said, hey this is Cornwall, how about a Cornish pastie – this pastie about a foot long, five inches high and five inches wide. And the hotel clings to the side of the rock and outside was this four-masted schooner sitting in the bay. There was a lady who lived there who had been foreign correspondent for *The Times* or something and her husband had been assassinated in Albania. And I was playing my autoharp in the bar late at night and she said: 'Can you play any Strauss waltzes?' 'Don't know, never tried.' So off we went with some waltzes.

The cider down in the West Country is amazingly strong and doesn't half make you fart. Not only that but it makes you mad, too. I got completely legless in St Ives on just two pints.

I had a wonderful room in a hotel in Norwich, the Queen Anne suite or something. It was a fifteenth-century affair. Or so they told me. The floor at each corner doesn't bear any resemblance to the floor at any other given corner. The angle of the floor is like waves. It's got big timber beams and a four-poster bed which is at least four feet off the ground so you have to get into it up a little spiral staircase. I was there the day John Lennon got killed. I was performing that night and I felt so sad and didn't really feel like going on. And halfway through it I told the audience that I felt depressed because of what had happened and everyone clapped because that was how every-one felt.

When we were in Workington on the tour we met a bloke there at the stadium, which is this sort of corrugated iron affair. He was telling us about what the town used to be like. It was very sad. 'There's no industry here,' he said, 'no business . . . and they don't even mention us on the weather reports any more.' It was such a wistful thing to say; as though he felt the weather people thought: Well who gives a fuck if it's raining in Workington?

Blackpool is always great when you're not there in the season, so you don't get the funny-hat people, just like the locals and the people who work in the boarding houses. It's great at that off-season time because you're selling out everywhere which means a lot for a comedian, to have a full house. You can be twice as funny to a full house — there isn't that jarring ego-letdown that goes with a half-empty hall.

Croydon I remember because I tore the backside of my trousers there.

And Buxton was a good one because we weren't talking to the press. There were a lot of weird things being written about me at the time and we thought — Bollocks. So we only spoke to school magazines and hospital radio. The school magazine questions were so good — they'd obviously sat down in a wee committee and said: 'You ask him this' and 'You ask him that'. And they took pictures with Instamatics. And on the way out the blokes from the nationals were trying to inverview the schoolkids . . .

And we'd get students along as well in the university and college towns . . . What I've always found extremely puzzling about 'University Challenge' is that on the one hand you get these very bright people up there who can tell you the first name of the bloke that built the fifth brick from the left on the south side of the main pyramid and then at the end you see them holding up this great big teddy bear mascot and waving its arm. Very odd.

But one of the oddest places we visited was the Channel Islands. A lot of retired folk go there so they have the number of a priest by your bed in case you need to get him to pop round and give you the last rites. They had a special door at the back of the hotel for taking the stiffs out through.

We had the car nicked on the road too but not in a very dramatic fashion. I like the story – true – about the guy who stole someone's car in London. The following day he puts it back outside their front door with a wee note in it: 'Terribly sorry to have taken your car but it was an emergency. I enclose two tickets for *Evita* for tomorrow night as an apology and a thankyou.' Great . . . the next night they go off to see *Evita*. Come back – their house has been completely cleaned out.

The police in all the wee towns often drop round to the show and to the dressing room – it makes a change for them from looking for burglars in boarding houses. They still like that song I do about bent policemen – it's amazing that I've been to court about three or four times and each time they've lied about what happened – so no wonder no one takes them seriously. And the first thing Thatcher did when she came to power was to up the salaries of the police and the army – so at least everyone knows where she's at.

You also bump into some funny clubs. There used to be an amazing one up in Glasgow where people like Charlie Drake performed and had to spend much of their time having their photo taken with the punters.

And there's this story about Matt Monro – which he tells himself – playing one of the clubs in Yorkshire, one of those out of the way working-men's clubs up there. But he can't find the club at all and stops off in a wee town to ask the way. So he flags down a cab driver and says where's this club? 'Aye . . . well, you drive out of town, turn left at the bridge, down a long hill, past a big garage, take a first right, carry on for about a mile and you'll see a big building on the left that looks like a supermarket. That's the club. But you don't want to waste your time there – that little creep Matt Monro's on this week.'

In Liverpool we wandered into an Indian restaurant and bumped into this great black guy who insisted on sharing his wine with us and asking me if I'd ever thought of getting dread-locks – either the full lot or if you're shy just the underarm hair. Why not?

God knows what they thought when Michael Heseltine went up there to sort people out. It must have been hilarious . . . but I like

Liverpool a lot. It's like Glasgow in lots of ways – they still have people hanging around chatting on the streets . . .

And those great big women that I always remember from my childhood who would be leaning out of the window watching the world go by . . . 'Aye, that looks like the world going by again . . .' I always used to imagine them with bare arses and the electric fire on.

Liverpool's also one of the tolerant places, not the sort of place where you run into trouble with the local clergy and the Whitehouses . . . They did a reading of 'The Romans In Britain' at the Glasgow Citizens – the play that Mary Whitehouse made all that silly fuss about. And when it was being done in Glasgow apparently she sent up a representative. So I wrote a letter to Giles Havergill at the Citizens saying 'How dare you sully these hallowed boards with this filth. I never dreamed you would sink to this level of depravity in the name of culture.' And I put my name at the bottom. I got this letter back – 'Sing about that,' it said – and I thought: Oh, fuck, he's taken me seriously. So I fired off another letter saying: sorry, you've taken me serious and I thought I was being glib and funny. Got another letter back from him saying 'I thought *I* was being funny when I wrote to you . . .'

It's funny the unexpected places you run into trouble. Ipswich: Radio Orwell banned 'Tell Laura I Love Her' because they said that the 'lyrics are a bit strong for folk in East Anglia'. . . . The best way to sell an album is to break up – but I can't do that, because I'm only me. I've never run into any problems with Mary Whitehouse. I think I'm on the telly too late at night for her.

You can't get away with too much early in the evening . . . like 'Crossroads'. Noele Gordon of 'Crossroads' was like royalty – I was at some do where she was and you couldn't smoke until she left. She announced herself by saying that 'Crossroads' was watched by sixteen million people every day. Then Dennis Waterman, who's also there, shouts out: 'I demand a recount!'

I was on 'This Is Your Life' and there is no feeling on earth like the one you get when someone you don't like walks out from behind the screen. Errrgh. Your face in that fixed smile. 'Heeello.' If you ever see a video of it – try to spot the one that owes me money.

- Steve Bell -

SOUTH AFRICA

have never been to South Africa and I imagine I'd be about as welcome there as a French kiss at a family reunion. They banned my last book for being morally degenerate, which is like being called boorish by an Australian.

Still a lot of people knock the South African government without knowing what they're talking about. So I'd like to list in the rest of this chapter some of the decent things they've achieved.

Belfast

Dublin

Limerick

Cork

IRELAND

t would be nice to be one of those mohair-suited comedians. Just put the suit on and tell Irish jokes.

But Ian Paisley has me terrified . . . You can't see the bolt at the back of his neck for the clerical collar.

His wife went to the dentist the other week. The dentist asked her: 'Well, how's the mouth?' 'Still in bed.'

And he goes on about: 'I haav five hondred men with firearm certificates!' Who cares? Have you ever been hit by a firearm certificate? It's as good as throwing meringues at a brick wall.

Paisley was out walking once. There was a spring in his step – he was walking on water. And he fell in. And just as he was going under for the third time he felt two arms underneath his armpits pulling him out. A young man had saved his life! So, after he's been all dried off and everything, Paisley says: 'Yong man, you haav saved my life. Is there something I caan do for you to repay you?' 'Well,' says the young man. 'You can make sure that I'm buried with full military honours.' 'That's a very strange request, yong man. Why do you ask for a burial with full military honours?' 'Welll . . . Mr Paisley. My name's Seamus O'Shaunessey. I come from the Falls Road. And when my father finds out what I've done he'll murder me!'

He calls himself a Reverend but I think it's a title from one of those colleges in America that you just send two dollars and you get a dog-collar sent back.

I got invited to a party in Belfast, an actress friend called Maggie Shevlane. I said: 'Suuure.' We were in the Europa and it's the most bombed hotel in Europe. They keep telling you this and eventually you get a bit jittery. And it's stockaded and barricaded at the front, people in flak jackets. It's a bit off putting . . . This party was around four in the morning because it was after the show and by the time I got there I was knackered and I stayed the night, sleeping in a chair, and wandered back in the morning. Jamie, my roadie, was in a state of cold panic. He'd gone to my room and it hadn't been slept in and he didn't know who to tell and what to tell them back at the office – 'Er, bad news, Harvey.' And he was muttering away about it, saying he should have watched me. When eventually I came back I was wearing a bright green jacket and I was on the road talking to three soldiers in the parachute regiment and they were saying: 'Is it true you used to be a para?' And there was a Royal Ulster Constabulary bloke getting an autograph for his wee daughter and in the middle of this Jamie saw me in the bright green, the biggest target in Belfast, and panicked again.

Later, after the tour was over, I went for a fishing contest in Fermanagh, which was Bobby Sands' constituency. It was very close to the time he was dying from his hunger strike and the TV people who'd arranged the competition thought it would be a good idea not to linger around where we didn't really belong. So we drove off to Dublin. Whoosh. And off back to London.

The following morning, back in London, we found out that the plane we *should* have been on – because we took an early one out – had been hijacked to Le Touquet by the Mad Monk. He was an Australian monk, as far as I can recall, with a bottle of vodka round his neck. God knows what would have happened if I'd been on board. Apparently he was a very nice guy – the passengers were saying: 'Aye . . . he was baby-sitting for my daughter, he was very good to us.' He wasn't your hard-nosed 'take-me-to-Havana' type, he was only after the secrets of Fatima.

He said that the Vatican were keeping it secret and it should be shared with the whole world – because apparently there were other Fatima secrets and when they were revealed, they were exactly true. But there's this third secret and it's kept in a vault somewhere in the Vatican and they show it to every new Pope. Probably it says something like: 'Put your money in Fiat', or some equally handy piece of advice.

I met a big man, an RUC man who'd been shot in the head twice. He'd gone to someone's door – a rebel fellow – and the bloke had seen him coming. As he got to the door he had the strangest feeling that all was not well and for some reason leant backwards. The rebel shot through the door as he was falling backwards and the bullet went straight through his hat, taking hair and skin and everything. The guy realised he was falling and the second shot was lower but it just nicked him as well.

His name I won't tell you – partly because I can't remember it and partly because just before I was due to go on stage he showed up with a wee bottle of tonic water for me. I said: 'Thanks very much', and thought: This is a bit odd, bringing someone a bottle of tonic as a present.

But it was potheen or poteen or potcheen or however you spell it which had been seized by the police and there was some in the station. He said: 'Take a wee drop before you go on.' And I said: 'No, I never do.' But I was totally and absolutely exhausted, the big black eyes stage. Knackeroni. And he said: 'I'll tell you what . . .' Took the top off the wee bottle – and you know how tiny they are – half filled a wee glass and gave it to me. I got the most sensational lift and it was one of the best gigs I've ever done.

We did two shows and so didn't come off until two in the morning and it was great because the police were coming up and saying: 'It's lovely watching people walk the streets of Belfast and retelling your stories. It's like the Belfast I knew when I was a boy.'

I didn't drink the rest of the potheen. We went back to the Europa and I told Zoot Money I had it and Zoot did the lot. I said: 'You must try this.' 'Sure.' Poured the lot into a tall glass and scoffed the lot. It had absolutely no effect at all. But Zoot can drink a bit. If I had done the same I wouldn't be able to write home.

People say that the folk in Northern Ireland are starved of entertainment and that's why they're a good audience. But I think they're a good audience because they're a good audience. In Bangor in 1982 we had a wonderful gig, the people were so friendly. The support act was a nice wee lot – 'Fine Girl You Are' kind of songs – and they had a flute player. I wanted to ask him where he learnt to play it . . .

When I did the concert in Belfast the last time someone in the audience shouted out: 'Great show, Billy, but what about the boys in H-block?' But I didn't feel I was there to stir things up and then run away. I'm there to give people fun. As it happens I believe in what the republicans want – that the Brits should get out and that if anyone from the North wants to come and live over here then that's fine. And the H-block people should have political status because if they've been arrested under a political law and tried without a jury, then it's political. But they lost my sympathy a bit when they put a bomb in a hall where I had played – they did apologise afterwards because they didn't think I'd still be there.

In Dubai we met a black Irishman so I was telling him what Phil Lynott said when he was asked how it felt to be black and Irish: 'Well, Guiness is black and Irish, isn't it?'

The record for someone drinking pints of Guinness is fifty-eight in one hour after which the bloke had a few drinks with his pals and walked home. I still haven't found out the record for hard-boiled eggs up the bum but I'm sure it's equally impressive.

At Phoenix Park in Dublin we had the traffic stopped for us by a drunk wearing a funny hat – you know the kind of bloke, trousers hanging down, a bit of bum showing, the lot. He leans into the car window breathing fumes and says: 'Have you anything, Billy, for a man?' So I said: 'I trust it's not for strong drink,' and gave him a fiver. He was so pleased that he stopped all the traffic for us like a policeman.

The last time I was in Ireland we did some 'charitable' things – visited an old folks home. And after it I got this smashing letter from a Mrs Robertson: 'Dear Billy, thank you very much for your charitable visit to our old folks home and for the presents you gave to the residents. I got a transistor radio, and I really treasure it, because I share a room with a Mrs McPherson. She has a radio but she always kept it really low so that only she could hear it and would never let me listen even when 'The Archers' – of which I'm very, very fond, – were on. But your radio has saved all that, for which I'm very, very grateful. Thanks very much. Mrs Robertson.
P.S. I came into the room yesterday and Mrs McPherson's radio had broken down and she asked if she could listen to mine. So I just told her to Fuck Off.'

- Steve Bell -

HONG KONG

think some people have a slightly odd idea about me because when I was in Hong Kong they kept saying to me: 'Oh, you'll be off to the topless bars tonight.' And I'd be saying: 'No, it's not my gig, I don't like that.' They didn't believe me – it was all: 'Oh, come on, you'll enjoy it, it's great down at the topless.'

It's the aftermath of that Rest and Recreation plan for the American troops in Vietnam – they messed up Bangkok in the same sort of way. Apparently before then it wasn't like that.

The thing that fascinated me in Hong Kong was the incredibly busy brothels. But it wasn't prostitutes using them – it was married couples who couldn't have it off at home because they were eleven to a room. It was granny and grandad and Uncle Willie and his two kids and you and the wife and your four kids all in the one room.

So at the weekend the guy would go into the brothel with his wife, have a cuddle and then go home. The beds are never cool. There's something very wise about that because it means that love-making becomes a big thing. You have to get up and get yourself ready and go to a place. It's a lot better than it being the last household chore of the day.

There's a lot of Scottish blokes in the Hong Kong police force – which was in a bit of a mess when I was there because of the bloke who had just shot himself three times in the back – and they have a bit of the Sanders-of-the-River thing about them.

The Army is a bit of an odd audience – they're nice enough guys but they're a bit schoolboyish. They got a bit out of hand so they sent down a colour sergeant, with the waxed moustache, the whole bit, your actual regimental sergeant major type. He was almost ordering them to laugh – but he saved the concert. If they were getting out of control you would hear this 'whuuff' – like a dog barking – and they would settle down. The previous night I'd almost walked off because it was so heavy and over the top – real head-in-the-soup time but he managed to make it normal.

But I was obviously pretty riveting – the guy operating the sound controls fell asleep. Which is not quite as bad as what happened in

Dubai – the guy who worked the lights there moved them around so much I think he must have worked at Colditz.

It was sad, though. One night when I arrived to do the show a guy had just died on the steps outside: an old Chinese guy with a bowl of noodles beside him and someone just lifted up his body and put him in another doorway.

My driver there was a Chinese lady called Lorretta who told me I had 'rubbery regs' – she said 'I thought you were angry person but I saw the show and you were rubbery.' I have this image of myself now as a piece of Dunlopillo. The concert was called 'Billy Connolly Brings The House Down' because I was the last act there before they pulled it down, which seemed a pity as it had that atmosphere of seedy colonialism about it.

The army boys in the audience were into a bit more heavy sexy stuff which I don't do but I don't like that stuff or racist stuff so it just has to stand or fall on its own.

One of the great things that will be with me till the day I die – along with the Arab dancing in his full regalia when I was playing the banjo in Dubai – was this Chinese guy in the audience who I just caught sight of, taking his glasses off to wipe his eyes and laughing hysterically. A lot of people tell you that the Chinese don't have a sense of humour. Total bullshit. I don't think there's a race on earth that don't have a sense of humour.

I never made it into China, to my regret, although I was with a bunch of guys from the Freightliners – or Frighteners I think they're known as because there's no furniture or anything inside these planes and they look a bit bloody terrifying – did ask me if I wanted to go up to Peking with them. You can't get off the plane and get your passport stamped – you just have to look out the window so it's a bit tantalising. But the cloud base was low so we said Forget it – you could be as well over the Isle of Wight.

There's a great business with Luck in Hong Kong. When you're building your house you get a guy in to advise you on where to place your bits and pieces for the best luck, to get the luck flowing through it, which is a nice concept. If the building's already built and you call him in, he'll tell you where to put your furniture. In Hong Kong the English people poo-poo the idea – but do it. I met one banker there who said his desk was in a really weird position in his office but he daren't move it. They do the same when they bury their dead, position them so that the luck is flowing through them, which is OK for the dead folk.

The Chinese came into the Gorbals before the Jews and there's still a big Chinese community in Glasgow, with a wonderful gambling fraternity in the midst of it.

Another luck thing they have in Hong Kong is I think, a power station there with five chimneys and one's false, because five is lucky and four isn't. I could, of course, have got the figures the wrong bloody way round.

There's a huge smuggling business – the junks they use cost a fortune. They borrow the money at the most extortionate interest rates and they pay it off in eighteen months, running Marlboroughs into South Korea. I thought it would be something like dope or stereos but it's American ciggies that's the big one.

I love it at night there. Suddenly the sky goes an odd colour and those gaudy paintings you see of Kowloon in Chinese take-aways become understandable. Those punters who paint on velvet on Bayswater Road have got it dead right – that orangey-black colour the sky takes on. People go a lovely colour as well.

The food's extraordinary but the live food put me off – prawns, lobsters, fish all swimming around and you're meant to point at the one you want. But I get a weird trauma about doing that, sentencing the poor bugger to death so I'd just ask for fish – which is no better morally.

Hong Kong is the most different place I've every been. It was a very pleasant shock. I used to go on little walks during the day as is my wont. You would see little alleyways – like the washhouses in Scotland behind the tenement buildings where you'd wash the bed-linen on a Monday. And you would see guys with wee trolleys and a mast on top of them and one I saw had about thirty Cartier belts, which they had been making in the alleyway, absolutely perfect.

The Hong Kong Burns Club do always ends up as a huge bun-fight apparently. All these Alistairs and Nigels and Henrys throwing tables across the room and having Good Fun. The dirtier the material, the more they were into it. Fuck Burns – let's have the Ball of Kirriemuir. There was too much Alistairishness around for me.

There are a lot of Gurkhas out there and a pal of mine was telling me how he'd been doing the whole hippie bit in India and Nepal and he'd been wandering through the Himalayan foothills and came across a wee village where he stopped at a stall for a cup of tea. And the guy who served him broke into this broad Glasgow accent – 'Jags for the Cup' and everything. It turned out he'd been a Gurkha and had lived in the Maryhill Barracks. Which has got fuck all to do with Hong Kong but never mind.

This is *not* a dope deal taking place in a Hong Kong hotel room.

PRINCIPAL EXPORTS:

BIG SHEEP

LITTLE SHEEP

MEDIUM SHEEP

Darwin

Townsville

Alice Springs

Brisbane

erth

NULLARBOR PLAIN

Iron Knob

Sydney

Adelaide

Canberra

Melbourne

AUSTRALIA

he Australians, for some reason, tolerate Scots. They find us a bit peculiar, I think, not quite sure what they press to make us work. But they can't stand English people.

They have a safari park there with a notice outside it that says: 'Englishmen on bicycles admitted free'. Legend has it that an Australian was driving through this park with his wee son to see the lions and tigers and everything. They came to the part of the park where all the lions hung out and there was one lion licking another lion's bum. And the wee boy said: 'Dad, what's that?' 'Well, son, the lion at the back has just eaten an Englishman and he's trying to get the taste out of his mouth.'

In a way you can understand them getting pissed off with all the expatriates: I was in a shop in Sydney, a fruit and vegetable place, and there was a Scottish woman in front of me in the queue. She's pointing at the fruit – you know they've got all these enormous grapes and lovely apples and things – and she's saying: 'Aye, ye cannae get fruit here like ye did in Scotland.' As if the grapes of Milngavie were legendary . . . the great Bute banana harvest . . .

When Tony Hancock went to Australia he was asked by immigration what he was going to do there and he said: 'I'm coming here to die.' And he did. They thought he was joking. You seem to meet a lot of funny people out there – I met Harry Secombe and Spike Milligan . . . they had a great traveller's joke in the Goons: 'I'd like a return ticket.' 'Certainly. Where to?' 'Back here of course, you fool.'

They're kind of coarse, Australians, until you get used to them. You arrive at the airport and it's: 'Hello, Bill, is this the wife – nice tits.' That sort of thing. But they are a perfectly balanced race: a chip on each shoulder. They're quite straightforward: 'Can I come up to your room for a coffee – or what I really mean is a meaningless fuck.' Nothing over-romantic. Ah . . . Australia . . . the jacaranda on the verandah.

And they produce some wonderful films, much better than anything that's happening in Britain. I loved *The Hills Have Eyes* – 'They came to find something different but something different found them'.

While I was with Parky in Sydney we had had a wee refreshment and I stopped a car at a traffic light and started making love to it. Then I did a wee soft-shoe shuffle past it. It was one of those occasions when you get so drunk you don't remember what happened and then people start telling you a little bit at a time and you're going: 'Oh, noooo, I diiidn't . . . Noooooo.' It's awful. But I don't believe this thing about the truth coming out when you're drunk. I've told people I loved that they really pissed me off and I've told people that I can't stand that I loved them. It's just rubbish that's jumbled up in your head and comes out.

What fascinated me about Sydney was King's Cross which is their sort of seedy area, all one-armed bandits and porn shops. And the people running them look *exactly* like they do in Soho and on 42nd Street in New York . . . it's not quite the same in LA, I think it's up some lane there and you can't see it, they've got it better organised – you can take part in an orgy and have a laugh. But all that seedy stuff intimidates me greatly for some reason, though I know it attracts some people enormously and I can see the fascination.

Tasmania is a bit like Guernsey. Very inbred. Full of weary willies. Everybody looks like the royal family. I think there must have been a lot of incest because they were short of people – incest's the game the whole family can play. Also known as 'roll your own'.

Dame Edna Everage sent me a bunch of gladioli when I was playing the Dallas Brooks Masonic centre – you had to be a contortionist to get in there because you had to do all those masonic gestures. I love Dame Edna's 'At least I can say I've been there' song. There was another song I liked out there, which was done by the woman who was on before me – 'I hate wogs, they eat bananas and they eat frogs' – it was a lovely sort of attack on all those feelings people have about foreigners.

Frank Ifield has just done a punk record. It's called 'I Remember You, Ya Bastard'.

The scene is Queensland, two little boys discussing their hobbies:
    'What do you collect?'
    'Um . . . I collect bees.'
    'Very good. How many bees have you got?'

'250,000.'

'And how many hives do you have for them?'

'Ten.'

'Well . . . I collect bees, too.'

'How many have you got?'

'A million.'

'A million bees! That's an awful lot of bees. How many hives do you have for them?'

'One.'

'But I've got 250,000 bees and ten hives for them. And you've got a million and only *one* hive for all those bees!'

'Fuck them.'

I love those non-jokes.

So here's another one: the time of the Royal Command Performance has come round and they've got all the acts queuing up for Bernard Delfont. Then one little bloke works his way into the Palladium and begs to have an audition.

'Well . . . what do you do?'

'I jump from the balcony and land on my head on a tin tray.'

'Very interesting. But we've got an almost full cast list and we really don't have enough time to see new acts.'

'Oh, please, *please*.' Begs away, and eventually they soften and allow him to show them his act.

Off he goes up to the highest balcony in the Palladium, perches on the lip of the balcony, hovers for a brief second and then comes plummeting down. And lands on his head right in the middle of his tin tray which is in the middle of the stage. Everyone is most impressed. But the guy clutches his head and moans . . . 'Oh . . . ah . . . oh . . . my head, my head . . .'

'What's the matter? Surely you're used to it?'

'No. I've never done it before.'

Why is that funny? They should have it as an 'O' level on humour.

The press there are quite an odd lot. I was on one chat show and the guy interviewing me asks: 'Well, Mr Connolly, how do you get your hair looking like that?' And this guy asking me is wearing a *wig*. So I said: 'I just do it and it points to the ground. How do you get yours looking like that?' Whoosh. On to the next subject.

On another programme they started off: 'What's your real name?'

They were a weird pair – they did that song 'Lady Di, Stick It in your Eye' and on their radio programme they told everyone on the Sydney Bridge to get out of their cars, do a wee dance and get back in again. And everyone did it. Traffic came to a standstill.

Not that I can have anything against chat shows. I half started off on one in Scotland – the 'Tennant Breakaway' or something like that it was called. I had to entertain between the two guests – usually they would have someone like an expert on the royal family and some handyman like a plumber to tell you how to fix your drains and I did a song in between. A wee while later they had a guest who took panic in the studio so I had to fill in there and tell jokes and I became a Personality.

Still, the press there were very sweet to me: one of the women writers had an article that went: 'Pamela Stephenson – with a face like that and a talent like that, she could be going out with Warren Beatty – so why is she hanging out with this Caledonian Yetti?'

The Australian hotels are pretty much like American ones, they all look the same after a while so I would just hang up the 'Do Not Disrobe' sign on the door and pass out.

Of course, you can always pop out of a night and grab a Dingo-burger. Or if you're in Melbourne, you can get a Dingo-in-the-Basket – very pleasant on a warm night with a coolish beer.

They get quite into the booze, over there. A pal of mine's brother came over from Australia to Partick and we took him off for a drink. Got into the bar, pints all round – only he helps himself to a pint glass, asks for a bottle of wine, pours the bottle into the glass and puts it away in one. I think he found us a bit boring.

For some reason, Australians abroad can get a bit obnoxious – they do it to places like Bali which used to be beautiful apparently but is now been made a bit naff in some places by all these people stopping off. Same with Bangkok – which is really a sort of exotic Blackpool – but it's been messed up by Australian reps going there for their hols.

I got beaten up on the stage in Brisbane. Which is quite a unique feeling – getting socked on the face in front of 3,000 people. It was a bad audience – I got booed on. I said: 'Gie's a chance to bore you first.' I was nervous – every hormone was standing on tiptoe . . . The guy who hit me was a Scottish-Australian prison officer, a real Molotov cocktail of a mixture that, and I think he'd just learnt to walk upright that day. He came down the aisle like a man possessed and I'm standing there in tights and yellow banana boots. And it's a funny thing when you're on stage because nothing moves normally – unless I move it – so if someone comes on stage it's a very weird feeling. So this nutter comes on the stage and says: 'You . . . you . . . filthmonger.' And I said: 'That's pretty accurate. I have been known to tell the odd risqué story.' And he goes: 'FILTHMONGER!' So I said: 'You're repeating yourself now . . . come on, we haven't got all night.' 'My wife's ears are not GARBAGE CANS! We didn't come here to listen to filth like this!' 'Oh – where do you normally go?'

And then he resorted to violence and gave me one of those Dick Barton punches, the ones with WHOOOSH written behind them that start miles away and go Biff! But he made a mistake that a few people have made. He thought that my chin came to the end of my beard. But I am *not* Jimmy Hill. I came out of it quite well. The Glasgow hardman. Hadn't moved an inch. So I was doing a lot of the shoulder work and saying: 'Is that your best shot, pal?' swaggering about like the bionic degenerate. Then he said: 'No!' and nutted me one. I was away crying – it was blood and snotters everywhere. I was carried off by my roadies – sounds very painful doesn't it? 'He was carried off by his roadies.' And as soon as they grabbed me I got very brave again. 'Hey, let me get at the bastard!' Then someone phoned the police and they beat me up too – they saw this guy in tights and thought: English poofter, bam bam. I couldn't believe it. Brisbane's such a funny place. They must have fried brains or something. That's what comes of spending half your life upside down suspended by your ankles. There wasn't a dry seat in the house.

I'd like to do a concert that just had women in the audience. I've never had a woman come up to me and say, the way men do: 'I saw you on Parky the other night and I think you're a prat.' You look at a National Front demonstration and you don't see women on it – they've got more sense.

It's sad the way that TV took over from films. If they put a few million into it in Britain like they did in Australia, it could really take off. They say: 'Oh, no, it has to stand on its own two feet.' But when did a nuclear weapon last stand on its own two feet? They spend £3,000 million on it and they don't even know if it will go bang.

Though they had a season of British Beat films on and they were dire, those early English rock and roll ones. They all had middle-class actors saying: 'Let's have a rumble with these other chaps,' and clicking their fingers. David McCallum in *Violent Playground*! Old Ilya Kuryakin – he used to live up the road from me in Glasgow, in the posh bit. I remember him as a boy – he had a very distinctive face.

Ah, Showbiz . . . what is still one of my favourite acts is Evel Knievel jumping over Harvey Goldsmith's credit cards.

What do a pelican, an ostrich and the Inland Revenue have in common? They can all stick their bills up their arse.

We flew out of Adelaide on Emu Airlines. We were 5,000 feet up in the air before someone pointed out that Emus can't fly.

The place we were flying to was called Iron Knob, would you believe. And they had a lovely wee zoo there – very civilised. The kangaroos were so domesticated that they had three pens in their top pockets. A wee Bic and a couple of pencils.

Still, I must be fond of Australia. I wear the bloody place through my ear – well, I've got an earring in the shape of Australia. I'm looking for one for the other ear that I can hang upside down.

- Steve Bell -

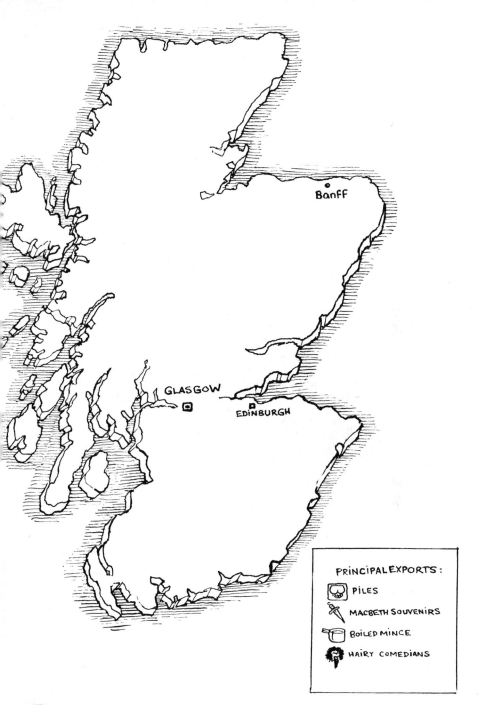

Banff

GLASGOW

EDINBURGH

PRINCIPAL EXPORTS:

PILES

MACBETH SOUVENIRS

BOILED MINCE

HAIRY COMEDIANS

SCOTLAND

One of the nicest things that ever happened to me was when I was working in the yards in Govan, this old welder and I were talking and I was telling him how I just wanted to get a banjo and go wandering around and be a hippie. And he said: 'Dae it now, son! Can you imagine what it'll be like when you're sixty with the rain running doon your neck, thinking you never did it?'

Those blokes were magic, one of the great things about Scotland. All the things that Scotland gets famous for are the nasty things: it's top of the league in Europe for numbers of people in prison per head of population, for cancer of the bum and for heart disease – but I think that last one's just because we're all so romantic.

And talking of romance . . .

There's an old couple, nice couple lying in bed. She's reading a book, the quilted dressing gown, everything. He's got the neatly pressed pyjamas, the hanky in the top pocket, he's just lying there passing the time . . . 'Toot-tee-toot' . . . She's just finished her chapter, puts the marker in the book and puts it on the bedside table. 'Remember,' he says, 'remember when we were a wee bit younger . . . and we used to make love?' 'Oh, aye.' 'Wellll . . . I was just thinking . . . we haven't done it for a long time, have we?' 'No . . . no, I suppose we haven't.' 'It got a bit boring, really, didn't it?' 'Aye, I suppose it did . . .' 'I was just reading that magazine *Forum* – one of the blokes at work had it – and they've got some interesting things in there that you can do.' 'Aye?' 'Well, I don't know – they sound quite interesting anyway . . . I was wondering if, maybe, we could try one – just a very simple one.' 'Uh-huh.' 'Well . . . there's one very simple one where you just . . . er . . . kiss the other person's bum.' 'Whaaaat?' 'Well, that's what it says. Apparently it's quite nice. Shall we try it?' 'You're having me on are you – you're going to take a picture for your mates or something?' 'No, no . . .' 'Well, I'm a wee bit embarrassed so can we have the lights out?' So he gets out of bed, puts out the lights, bangs his shin on the table as he comes back – oooo – gets in under the blankets at the bottom of the bed and kisses her on the bum. 'Was that nice?' 'Aye – that was quite nice,' she says. 'It's my turn now.' 'Aye – don't worry about the lights, I'm no' shy.' So she gets up, puts the light on, back to bed, lifts up the blanket. He's on his knees with his pyjama bottoms down waiting for her to kiss his bum. Nothing happens. Waits a minute. Nothing. Then she says: 'It's a crying shame – all those people killed in that earthquake in Peru.' 'Jees – what brought that on?' 'You've got a bit of the *Daily Mirror* stuck to your arse.'

Phlegmatic race. A great pal of mine Hamish Imlach was booked to perform in Crieff. It was one of those, you know the kind – well, I hope you do – public parks with a little bandstand. So Hamish turns up and sees the promoter, Archie. 'Hello, Archie, how you doin'?' 'OK.' 'Many here tonight?' 'Och, not really. Perhaps it's the rain kept them away.' 'Never mind, we'll away out and do twenty minutes.' So he walks out with his guitar. One guy in the audience! And the rain is walloping down. And there's just this one guy with the Packamac on. So Hamish does his twenty minutes. Then he says to the guy who's sat through the rain and listened: 'Look – I'm going in for a drink, d'you want to come?' And the fellow in the Packamac says: 'Aye – but don't be too long – I have to put the chairs away.'

I used to play a lot of those wee social clubs when I was a folk singer. The kind of places where the committee rules everything. One time I was at the Grinton Steel Social Club waiting in the wings with my guitar. The head of the committee gets up to the microphone – it's always one of those microphones that distorts everything . . . 'Will the owner of car number beeesen-aysshh-hawww-fiiinnne-sissss-oooo please' and so on. They often have them at bingo games: 'The winner is number hay-hem-hi.' Everyone's looking at their tickets. Anyway. The head of the committee taps the microphone and says: 'Eh, we've had a number o' complaints about peepil pissin' in the car park. Now the committee has just forked out four hundred pounds on new toilets last year so there's no need for peepil tae piss in the car park and folk gettin' their feet wet gawn tae their cars in the dark. It's a damned disgrace – having tae wade through piss and the committee is well sick o' it. So cut it oot. Right – Billy Connolly.'

They're amazing these committee men: 'We've had complaints aboot the acoustics so we've put doon traps . . . Ye'll see next week's guest pinned tae the door . . .'

The committee were like the Mafia or the masons or something. They ran everything and what they said went. They were into all the dodges and the fiddles and everything. First prize in a raffle would be a holiday for two in Majorca. Second prize would be a week on the committee, which would probably be more profitable. And they would hang onto your money until you'd finished and always time you to make sure that you didn't do less time than what they were paying you for.

And one thing the MC's would do – if you were a comedian and some of the punters were talking a bit during your act – is, *just* as you were coming to your punchline, they'd stand up and say very loudly: 'Hey, *c'mawn* – gie the man a chance!'

They would always be very proud of their *facilities* – the toilets and the PA and everything and they would let you know exactly how much they'd cost.

The toilet in the Victoria Halls, Campbeltown, is just behind the stage and there's a notice in there which says: 'Do not flush during performance' and some local wit has crossed out the 'u' and put in an 'a' so it reads: 'Do not flash during performance'.

Ages ago when I was performing there they made me have a Gaelic choir as an opening act. They were great and it went down a storm but at the end of it they turned out to be rare wee twisters and they tried to get me to pay more money. It was all: 'D'ye not think we went down very well there? How about an extra fifty quid . . . I'm sure another fifty wouldn't hurt you . . . you could write it off against your tax.'

That was the night we had Pastor Jack Glass outside as well, and the Rangers supporters inside because Campbeltown isn't exactly the home of liberal thinking in Scotland, it's where a lot of the bombs to Northern Ireland come from. Remember those mysterious blowing ups of fishing boats? 'The boiler exploded,' they'd explain – the fucking boat was in splinters from here to the Isle of Man.

There were a lot of bluenoses in the audience. It was very, very alive and they were shouting and bawling and I was shouting and bawling. I had to get a police escort out of town because someone put all my tyres down. I'm sure it was Jack Glass's mob – so that they could get a bit of a shout at us. I half expected him to show up in London when I said I was going to do the crucifixion. It was nice to do it again after all those years. It proved I was right to drop it. It was good in the sense that it got me an audience that wasn't folkies in those days when I was starting but I'm glad I didn't get stuck with having to perform it every time like it was Tony Bennett and 'I left my Heart in San Francisco'.

Springburn is another place that sticks in the memory. Poor Springburn . . . They eventually rolled it up and sold it to Zambia – the kids are still playing in the streets in their wellies wondering why it's not raining yet.

Glencoe has a hotel with a sign in it that says: 'No hawkers or Campbells'. And I met a great American woman called Mary Campbell, a really nice woman. And in the course of events she was introduced to someone called – really – Wilma Cakebread. And Wilma Cakebread says: 'I never shake hands with a Campbell.' So Mary says: 'Personally, I don't think I'd marry the first Mr Cakebread I met.'

There's a guy called David Webster from Oban who does a summer show. Kenneth McKellar and him. He does the whole thing with slides. It's just him and his slides and people turn up for it in droves. He's got a wee photography shop in Oban and he sets off on the road with the slides. I'd love to see him because I gather he's a real ham. Slides of the Falls of Muchart. When I played the Free Trade Hall in Manchester for the first time he was the coming attraction and I'd love to see who he attracts.

The Highlands are getting that NATO base whether they like it or not. But a lot of them up there are Wee Frees so if there's a war on a Sunday, we've had it anyway. 'Ohhh, nooo, not on the Sabbath.'

Stornoway I always remember from school because Ecclestone Institute, Stornoway, would always win 'Top of the Form'. They've got some intake to university from that school. I think it's the desperation to get off the island.

Our school was on 'Top of the Form' but it got thrashed – total humiliation. And me and the lads who were in the technical bit were all going: 'Oh-ho-ho-ho – saw you getting fucked last night.' It was great to get back at those brainy bastards.

137

I was on 'The Kenny Everett Show' – full Highland dress, the sword, everything, in an ice-cream parlour. And the guy who's serving me in the wee white jacket is David Frost . . . 'Yes, Can I help you?' So I come in and go up to the counter to order. And he goes: 'Sorry – we don't serve Scots.' 'Whaat?' 'We don't serve Scots – it's the policy of the company.' 'I don't believe this. I want to see the manager immediately.' And the manager comes down the stairs. It's Kenny Everett in full Highland regalia. 'Yes?' 'What's all this – you don't serve Scotsmen?' 'Have you tasted the ice cream?'

Remember all that cannabis washed up on the Isle of Mull? The police say that a lot of it was never found and that some of it got eaten up by the sheep – but I think the Mull farmers are a wee bit smarter than that . . .

The greatest way for travelling in the Highlands was the SMT buses, the green ones, there was something romantic about them and they were what you would take when you went off camping. But all that rubbish about camping building the character – it did nothing of the sort. It just made your knees wet. Not that we used to go with a haversack and things – we went with a plastic mac, a bottle of wine and a spoon, in case we met someone with a can of beans. And we would take our own bus stop – made out of beer cans stuck together: you'd shove it down on the road, the bus would stop and you'd take it on the bus with you – this is round Loch Lomond because there were no bus-stops round there. And sometimes we would go down into the Loch itself – stand up to our waists in the water, looking like a queue. It was a great hit with the tourist buses who would come round the corner and see us – 'Fuckin' 'ell, take a look at that!'

The Glasgow buses are less romantic –
  'Hey, pal, is this bus for Drumchapel?'
  'Naw.'
  'But it says Drumchapel on the front.'
  'It says India on the tyres but we're no' gawn there either.'

A couple from Partick win the pools. Never had any money in all their life. So they buy a house and move out to Bearsden. Thought it was a nice view. Their neighbours are none too happy – take the dogs inside and everything. So the couple decide they'll go off on a cultural tour to improve their minds.

They get back a couple of months later and get in touch with their friends: 'Well, we had a crackin' time . . . We went tae Chopin's house. He wasnae there – probably out daein' a message or somethin' . . . if he'd been in I'm sure it would have been straight in, cup o' tea, feet under the table . . . Then we went tae see the Mona Lisa. That was OK but it was very small. And then . . . oh, aye . . . then we went tae Galway tae see the very organ that had been used by . . . hey, Jean, what was the name o' that cunt that wrote Handel's Messiah?'

There was a woman at a bus stop in Partick and this very shaggy dog came up and pissed over her leg. So she takes a biscuit out of her shopping bag and drops it on the ground for the dog. And her friend says: 'What are ye daein' that for?' 'So's I can see which end it's head is so that I can kick it up the arse.'

The Sheriff's Courts in Glasgow are always strange places to visit . . . when there's a really horrible case on, the public gallery is always packed.

There is a guy in the dock in Glasgow – a real filthy revolting character. The public gallery is full because they love a really dirty case. And they're all going – 'Ye filthy dirty bastard pig!' 'Silence in court.' Anyway, he's up on some terrible charges: interfering with snails, feeding people sweeties that he's put up his bum, sucking budgies . . . The judge looks at him sitting there in the dock – he's scratching himself and sort of snorting. The smell is devastating. And the judge says: 'There is no doubt at all in my mind that you are the dirtiest, filthiest, most repellent creature that I have ever had the misfortune to pass judgement on. Do you have anything at all to say in your defence?'

'Fuck all.'

The court is in uproar. People swoon in the public gallery. The judge goes purple. His wig's all skew-whiff and his glasses are down over his nose. Finally he leans over to one of the clerks in front of the wee podium.

'*What* did he say?'

The clerk leans over to him: 'He said "Fuck all", your honour.'

'Funny . . . I could have sworn his lips moved.'

A Glasgow sheriff asked a woman why she shot her husband with a bow and arrow: 'Because I didnae want tae wake the kids.'

I always remember one wake I was at in Glasgow. We were all in the house, all the people who'd known the bloke and all his relatives. And this guy who I didn't know popped his head round the door and said: 'I'm the corpse's brother – would you like a drink?' Though I've heard there's more fun at a Glasgow funeral than at an Edinburgh wedding.

But the great thing about the way Glasgow is now is that if there's a nuclear attack it'll look exactly the same afterwards . . . I was abroad when all the riots were going on and people asked why Glasgow didn't have one. But they did – it was on Friday evening and nobody noticed the difference.

The weather's also unique. There are two seasons in Scotland: June and winter.

What I used to like about watching Jim Baxter play football on the telly was that you would see the whole of his face. With other players you would just see their profile, but with Jim Baxter – he would be watching the rest of the park, working it all out. There's very few players around like that nowadays who do things instinctively – Kenny Dalglish is one. The sad thing is that all those wonderful individualists get it all beaten out of them by the sort of people running the game so that now I'd rather watch Latin Americans than British teams, they've still got some of that left.

Scottish football was summed up for me by a game between Dumbarton and Dundee United on a really awful winter's day. It was all snow and sleet and cold and the poor goalie was soaking. He was taking his gloves off and shaking the water out of them. And he had to get the linesman to come over and wipe the mud out of his eye because he couldn't do it himself, his gloves were so muddy. Finally, the referee decides that he's going to abandon the match so he blows his whistle and waves them all off. All the players – except the goalie – run up to the ref and argue with him to let them finish the game. But the goalie's off like a bullet! He's in the bath while they're still arguing with the ref.

But one player that used to have all that skill and delicacy was Charlie Cooke. I remember him saying to me once that when Jim Holton passed the ball to him it had bruises on it.

There's this Celtic supporter and his friend at half time at Parkhead. And you know how important it is for them to know what's happening to Rangers at half time and how it's as important for Rangers to be losing as it is for Celtic to be winning. Anyway. These two blokes are in the gents' at Parkhead. One's trying to have a piss. He's got a pie in one hand, the Bovril in the other, he's got all sick down his jacket, his shirt's out of his trousers, booze spilt everywhere and he's trying to prop himself up so that he can have a piss. He gets his left testicle out and thinks that's it and starts peeing down his left trouser leg. So there he is: sick, piss, half-eaten pie – and he leans over to his friend and says: 'I wonder how the animals are gettin' on.'

A friend of mine was working in a bookie's in Highbury when Celtic were down for a friendly with Arsenal – Sammy Nelson's testimonial. And a Celtic supporter came in and said he wanted to put some money on Celtic. So the bookie told him that he was sorry, they didn't take bets on friendlies. 'Celtic doesnae play friendlies,' came the reply.

The Scots fans down at Wembley in the year when they were meant to be banned were amazing: there was one lot driving down had a wee sign in their car window that said 'Joe Jordan Boots Harder than Billy Connolly' and a whole lot stopping off on the motorway cafés doing that Scots fan bit: 'The English are all poofs and the beer's piss – there's only one way tae beat the English and that's twice.' Still, it was a lovely atmosphere when they all got there.

Pretty odd game. I've never seen a referee jump around so much, a French bloke called Wertz, he kept leaping in the air – at one stage I thought he was going to take the penalty himself. Why not?

Coming back from Wembley into London after the game there were those fans, the ones with nine tartans on – look like a Highlander designed by a committee – as though they belonged to every clan in the world. It was like Culloden only they were wearing silver platform shoes, Bri-nylon socks, Adidas running shoes. These weird people who had never seen a kilt before but now they had three on.

And when they saw me in the traffic they came running over, half-pissed and full of bonhomie; they started putting their bums into the taxi window for me to sign an autograph. And it's hard work trying to sign your name on those great big pink squidgy bums. So I ended up just putting a cross on each one of them – and one of them goes: 'Congratulations – you just won Spot the Ball.'

Watching all this was an English policeman doing the traffic duty. He couldn't believe what he was seeing – dozens of grown men lifting up their kilts so that a bloke in a car could write his name on their backsides.

I go sometimes to those dinners before the game when it's all jokes about the managers and the players. The story I like is told by Colin Welland, a great bloke incidentally, about Jackie Charlton becoming manager of Sheffield Wednesday. Charlton had said: 'I don't mind the fact that the manager's name is written in chalk outside his office – it's the wet sponge hanging beside it that bothers me.'

I often worry about ill parrots. Do they get sick as a football manager? I bet parrots feel awful when they get given a vote of confidence by the board.

What a job – at least players don't get messed around in quite the same way. And they can still go off to America and make a bit of money at the end of their careers in Britain: Willie Johnstone went off and joined the Boston Stranglers. One of my great favourites has always been Danny McGrain who gave me one of his Scotland jerseys – and it had on the label inside it: 'Made in England'.

Danny's an amazingly modest bloke for what he's achieved. I don't know if it's a thing that Scottish sportsmen have but I noticed when Jocky Wilson, the darts champion from Kirkcaldy, was interviewed on the BBC, at the end of his wee talk he said: 'I'd like to thank the BBC for having me,' like he'd been there for tea or something.

When I was a wee boy I read a football book by Neil Mochan, full of tips on how to play well, and it said that you had to learn to crack your leg like a whip. So I would wander around the streets with a ball trying to crack my leg like a whip. My dad saw me doing it and asked me what I was up to and I said: 'Oh, trying to crack my leg like a whip, Dad,' and he told me not to be so daft.

My poor dad once took me to the zoo in Glasgow and went off for a jar and came back and couldn't find me and thought I'd got lost. It was the day that Sheila the Tiger escaped. He thought I'd been eaten by her. Another time he lost me in the Barrowlands and a police-woman found me and took me to the police station and I got a sultana cake and sympathy.

He told me one wonderful thing, my dad: 'We all make mistakes – that's why you have a rubber on the end of your pencil.' Wonderful! Fuck all that 'Alas, poor Yorick' stuff, it's much over-rated. Now he says I look like a tramp keeking out of a hayloft.

Kids have this idea that they're told they'll be in school till they're sixteen. And I remember a wee boy going to school for the first time and asking his dad when he left him at the gates: 'Will you come back and pick me up when I'm sixteen?'

I left home very young. I was fourteen. But I came home. It got dark.

The scene in a Catholic primary school in Glasgow. The school-teacher is standing in front of the class.
    'Now boys and girls, today is a very, very important day in the history of this school, isn't it?'
    'Yesss, Miss.'
    'Now, Jeannie, could you tell the class what's so important about today?'
    'Yes, Miss. A real Cardinal is coming to see us all the way from Rome. And he's coming to our school because he used to be a pupil here.'
    'Very good. Now, Johnny, how do we address a Cardinal? Do we call him Father like a priest?'
    'No, Miss.'
    'Do we call him Your Grace, like a bishop?'
    'No, Miss.'
    'What do we call him?'
    'Your Eminence, Miss.'
    'Correct. Sit down, Johnny. We call him "Your Eminence". We must remember that. What do we call him, children?'

'YOUR EMINENCE, MISS.'

'Right. And I want you to be on your very, very best behaviour because this is a very important man. And your mothers have turned you out beautifully. You're *sparkling*.'

The magic moment arrives and there he is. Resplendent in vestments. The hat. The whole number. And he swishes into the room. Swoosh . . . 'Good morning, children.'

'Good morning, Your Eminence.'

'Sit down, children.'

And he hoovers across to the desk. (I always get the impression that the priests with those cassocks on have tricycles underneath. Or roller skates.)

The teacher goes: 'Good morning, Your Eminence. This is a great privilege and the whole class is delighted that you've chosen us.'

'Well, this was my old class.'

'Wonderful.'

'D'you mind if I speak to the children?'

'Not at all.'

He goes over to the first row: 'Hello, son, what's your name?'

'Francis Maguire, Your Eminence.'

'Hello, Francis. And what would you like to be when you're a big boy?'

'I'd like to be an engineer, Your Eminence.'

'Did you hear that, boys and girls?'

'Yes, Your Eminence.'

'Francis wants to be an engineer. That's a good thing isn't it?'

'Yes, Your Eminence.'

'Do you know why it's a good thing?'

'No, Your Eminence.'

'Well, I'll tell you. Because engineers look after the earth that God gave us. They derive energy from moving water. They build bridges. They make roads. Clever men. Sit down, son. Terrific.'

Moves along the row a bit to another wee boy.

'Hello, son.'

'Hello, Your Eminence.'

'What's your name?'

'Paul Murphy, Your Eminence.'

'What are you going to do when you're a big boy, Paul?'

'I'd like to be a plumber, Your Eminence.'

'A plumber?'

'Yes, Your Eminence.'

144

'Why do you want to be a plumber, Paul?'

'Because ma . . . ma . . . ma daddy's a plumber, Your Eminence.'

'Did you hear that, boys and girls?'

'YES, YOUR EMINENCE.'

'Paul wants to follow in his fathers footsteps.'

'Yes, Your Eminence.'

'Does that remind you of anybody?'

'No, Your Eminence.'

'What about Jesus?'

'Oh, yes, Your Eminence.'

'Well, don't forget again, will you? He's nailed to the wall to remind you . . .'

Meanwhile there's a wee boy in the front row, fiddling away.

'Connolly, what are you doing?'

'I'm lookin' for ma dinner money, miss.'

'Take your hand out of there, you liar, before you hurt yourself. And stop picking your nose.'

Of all the people in the class to pick, the Cardinal picks him.

'Hello, son.'

'Hi.'

'And what are you going to do when you're a big boy?'

'Aw – fuck off.'

Well, the scenes that followed hardly bear description. Sporadic fighting broke out in the back row. The teacher fainted. Legs up in the air. Big blue knickers.

'*What* did you say to me?'

'I said "Fuck off". Are you deaf as well as daft?'

The place was in an uproar. The teacher fainted again. Chairs went through the window. Fighting and noise everywhere.

'YOU HORRIED BOY! YOU REPULSIVE CREATURE! From under which stone did you crawl? I was a pupil in this very class! At that self-same desk sat I. But I didn't sit there interfering with myself, picking my nose and saying horrible things to guests. Nay. I sat down and worked and studied hard and won a scholarship to a posh school. I worked even harder, went to college and became a priest. Did I rest on my laurels? *No*. I worked *even harder*. Three years I was a parish priest. I worked and studied, worked and studied all the hours that God sent. I haunted the libraries of this land (underlining things and writing in the margin: "My thoughts entirely"). I was invited to the Sorbonne to study. They made me a canon. A monsignor . . . and a bishop. Five years later, I was an archbishop. STILL I STUDIED! I was invited to study at the feet of the Holy Father in the Vatican. They made me a cardinal. I WAS ON THE JURY WHO ELECTED THE LAST POPE. And *you're* telling *me* to fuck off? *YOU FUCK OFF!*'

I hated music at school. Our teacher was into those modern methods of instruction: grab you by the back of the neck and bang your head against the desk. She would make us do 'Three Blind Mice' with each row doing a different line. Chaos. Because we had this system of four rows. At the front were the bright boys with blazers who talked nicely and they got to sit nearest the windows; behind them were the sort of OK ones, in-the-middle type. The third row, where I was, was the Stupid But Saveable department. And behind us were the animals. They *shaved*. You know the kind – *born* with pubic hair. They all sat at the back with Mungo who was their boss. They used to charge protection money to get into school . . . 'Hey gie us that piece of toast . . . Gie us your dinner money . . .'

We had a girl at school called Lydia Tea. That's a lie actually but we did have a headmaster called Ribchester. How do you like that? They were going to ask me to give away the school prizes and then they saw one of my shows and thought better of it.

One piece of harmless fun we used to get up to was when this old bloke was singing in the street we would heat pennies up in the oven and then throw them to him.

I don't know if they do it in other British towns but in Glasgow when you're at school they take you away once a year to the countryside. You all get bundled into the bus and bundled out to the country.
    The teacher says: 'Right. See that green stuff over there?' – 'Yes, sir.' – 'Grass. And you see that brown and white stuff eating that grass?' – 'Yes, sir.' – 'Coos. Don't break them and be back here in half an hour.'
    Off you go wandering around, looking at the trees, wondering what to press to make them work . . . Well, this wee boy comes back to Glasgow after his day in the country. He's back at five in the evening and his dad's coming in from his work.
    'Hello, son.'
    'Hello, Dad.'

'How did it go today, the school trip and everything?'

'It was dead, dead good.'

'Aye, what did you do?'

'They gave us a bag of buns and a pork pie and we ate it and Harry Johnstone vomited oot the windae ontae this motorcyclist. . .'

'Aye – but what did you do in the countryside?'

'It was great. I loved it. We all got bundled off the bus and the teacher showed us things and he let us go a walk. And there was all coos and everything . . . And they were eating the grass and doing jobbies – at the same time! They're very clever, coos. And we went intae another field and it was all full of pigs. I didn't like them: they were farting and eating rubbish. Dead smelly. And we went up a wee lane and there was another field and we were asking the teacher questions – Miss, how can a horse dae that and still keep walking? That's clever, that. And this field was all full of chickens and the wee houses that they lived in. They were my very, very favourites. Then there was another field and that was all full of fuckers. Then there was a field over here with all sheep in it . . . And then there was a wee donkey and . . .'

'Hey . . . hey . . . wait a minute. D'you think we could go back a couple of fields?'

'What – the chickens? I liked them. They were my very –'

'No, no. I think it came after that.'

'Oh . . . the sheep?'

'No. I think the one before that.'

'Oh – the fuckers?'

'Fuckers, you say?'

'Aye . . . fuckers.'

'And what are fuckers when they're at home?'

'Welllll . . . the teacher said they were effers but *we* knew what she meant.'

When I was sixteen, a wee fair-haired boy, acne, I worked in the shipyards for a bloke called Sammy Boyd. And he was always trying to get rid of me – 'Oan ye go, son, awa' tae the lavvie.' I spent about five years in the lavvie. These lavvies were like something out of Dickens. The smell was horrendous. People had done obscene drawings on the wall and the years had gouged them into the wall so that even when the painters came and did them you could still see them. And I said to Sammy one day: 'These lavvies are disgusting, horrible places . . .' 'Luxury, son, luxury – ye should have seen them when I was a boy . . .'

According to him in those days there was no door on the cubicles for a start. Hence the popularity of the *Glasgow Herald*, which was – still is – a big paper. There were only half partitions between each lavvie so you could have a chat with the bloke next to you. No toilet seats as we know and love them: it was a bar, a wooden bar and you just hung on it like a budgie. And there were spikes sticking in the wall so that you couldn't lean back. The legs going dead, sitting like that. They didn't have bowls or anything like that. Just a long trough with constant running water . . . So that if the guy at the end did a wee jobbie it would come whooshing down. If the guy had had a curry the night before, everyone knew.

Apparently, the great game for apprentices was to bunch up a newspaper and light it and throw it in the trough so that it would float down ablaze – HELP! Big grown men leaping in the air with their pubic hair ablaze. But Sammy would say: 'They were hardy men in those days, son. They used to beat the flames oot wi' a *hammer*.'

The guys on the night shift at the yards were great, too. They were called Cole Porter – Night and Day.

They were great drinkers, too, and would have wonderful New Year's celebrations. That's the great thing that New Year has over Christmas – there isn't God around to knacker the proceedings.

I have a neighbour up in Scotland who is a *real* drinker. I like him because he makes me feel like a moderate drinker. His face is like Tenerife – cirrhosis of the face.

  Anyway, it's New Year's Eve and he takes his wife, who's a very wee woman, down to the pub. Now she doesn't drink so they get there and he says: 'What would you like?' 'Oh, I don't want anything . . .'

  'Come on – it's New Year's Eve! A wee drinkie-poo. A bijou drinkette. Won't harm you at all. You can have anything you want – except Avocat, because that looks like snot.'

  'Och,' she's really flustered, 'I don't know – I'll just have whatever you're having.'

So he orders – 'Two double whiskies' – a real chivalrous gent.

Now I don't know if you remember the first time you ever tasted whisky and the tremendous shock to the nervous system that it is. In Scotland this usually happens around the age of four – not because your parents give it to you but because there are these parties at New Year . . .

They have all the relatives crashing around knocking the crinoline ladies off the mantelpiece – 'Aw, no! We got that in Majorca!' – and everyone would be singing . . . 'Aye, remember your Uncle Bobby would sing that song he learnt in Malta . . .' Your Auntie Betty makes a fool of herself, doing the twist and falling all over the place . . . Your granny's in the corner – every time she leans forward the gin rolls out of her eyes.

Everyone's singing all those songs about being far away from Scotland. This is an extraordinary thing about Scots – they're always singing about missing Scotland when they're actually there . . . 'Though I am far away frae hame . . .' – 'Aw, shuttup. Ye're in the front room.'

Anyway – your relatives are all leaving their drinks lying around and not remembering where they put them. And you come in from the kitchen, aged four, bored stiff, full of sultana cake. And you see this wee glass with what looks like Irn Bru in it . . . 'Oh, Irn Bru fae Bill-bill.' Knock it back. YEUGGGHHHH!

You know that feeling – sometimes you get it when you drink a can of beer the morning after a party in the house . . . when you go around all the cans to see if any have got beer left in them. Shake them all. Empty. Empty. Then you find one with beer in it. Great! Whoosh. Knock it back. Someone's left a bloody fag end in it. You put it down like it was a white shark.

Well, the drink of whisky had that effect on the woman. 'AAARGH!' She spits it out. 'That's *disgusting*! How can you drink that *revolting* stuff?'

'There you are,' he goes. 'And you think I'm out every night *enjoyin*' maself.'

One Christmas they came up to the forest near Drymen to get the tree for George Square in Glasgow, the great big one with all the fairy lights and everything on it. So a team of blokes came out, found a tree the right size, a big forty-foot job, stuck it on the low loader and headed off for Glasgow. They were back the following day. 'Here again, eh?' 'Aye, we need another tree.' 'What was up with the one you got?' They had stopped at the traffic lights at Maryhill and some bastard had come out and sawed the first six feet off the tree, the top bit, so when they got to George Square the top was *square*. Somebody had obviously thought 'Aye, that'll do fine for the house . . .' Whack. Off he goes. Best tree in Maryhill.

There's a wee forest just north of Milngavy, a private estate, and some smart punter just set up a stall on a Sunday afternoon before Christmas, nicked a bunch of trees and sold them to the passing traffic. Two hours and he made a fortune – 'roll up, children half price' – he was off before anyone noticed their forest was down to half size.

It's partly to do with the time of year – this weird feeling of euphoria that takes the country over for a while . . .

Poor Matt McGinn. He died on 2 January having given up the booze. But there was no one around. Scotland was drunk. You think sometimes with things like that: Why didn't he call me? And then you think – Why didn't I call him? The worst thing is thinking about the person dying alone . . .

The rituals of drink have always fascinated me. The way curry has become a sort of traditional Scottish food after a night of drinking. I had pals in Glasgow who would – when they wanted to impress – get a take-away curry from somewhere like the Koh-I-Noor. Then before their friends arrive, they put it in pots in the oven. Then the pals get there and the host is tasting it, putting his head to one side, adding a wee touch of spices . . . 'Mmmm, could do with a wee bit more masala, I think . . .'

Though I do think it's amazing the way Scottish food has never been developed in a big way because the traditional Scottish foods are magnificent. Wonderful soups and fishes. And if you're into meat, that venison is rather jolly.

I cook a lot now. Who'd have thought that one day I'd be swapping recipes for profiteroles and soufflés? Who'd have thought that one day Shirley Williams might be Prime Minister? Some of my creations look a bit odd. Like The Thing That Ate Fulham. Or the Thing That Fulham Wouldnae Eat, more likely.

Beer and curry . . . but it's funny some of the names that bands have taken on: Free Beer is a great name. Looks good on the posters. And Late License was a Dundee band. You can see the punters: 'Late license, eh? Let's go on there then, eh?'

I bumped into one of the Bay City Rollers in London. It's funny how they've still not been accepted as a good band. People always used to make snidey remarks about them but when they played the Apollo in Glasgow, the audience loved it. The kids came out really happy. The next week they had Leonard Cohen there and everyone came out and jumped under the buses. Which was better?

It was like the folkie thing, too. How did we get away with it? Singing about dead lifeboat men – what a night out.

Not that there was all that much competition: Fran and Anna, Scotland's singing cruet set.

Still, I can talk. I've got a voice like a goose farting in a fog. And the autoharp I play is really just a thirty-four-string breadboard – dead handy for slicing tomatoes, too.

I was at one party in Springburn where there was a completely naked bloke lying in the coats room, farting and feeling himself up. And people were having to go: 'Er, excuse me, can I get to ma coat?' And he would just grunt: 'Awfuckawf!' One of the women came through to where the party was going on and told her husband: 'There's a man through there that was rude to me – told me to fuck off.' So her husband – a skinny bloke, built like a jockey's whip, a real cancer case, goes through. 'I'll see about this . . .' Slaps the drunk guy hard on his naked arse and says: 'What's this you've been saying to my wife?' The drunk gets off the bed, puts on one shoe, stands up, completely naked except for the one shoe and kicks the husband in the balls. Then he gets back on the bed and goes back to sleep.

Must be a Scottish trait that. I had a driving instructor, a great bloke, who taught me to drive. One time I was out for a lesson and there was a sports car behind us at the lights. And I had a job getting started and the guy in the sports car leans on his horn: WHAAAAAAAMMM. That awful sportscarry whine. A right prick. So my instructor got out of the passenger seat – we're down beside the docks – leans into the open sports car, takes the keys and throws them straight into the Clyde. Very satisfying.

There's also this thing in Scotland about successful musicians: 'Aye, him he's a poof – wears coloured claes – must be a poof. Long hair and pink suede boots – thinks he's Peter Pan.' You're supposed to have yellow skin and only ever be seen looking out of a bookie's doorway. Talk about Partick Thistle for the rest of your days. I was with a guy in London looking at the scores coming up on the television on a Saturday afternoon. And he said when Partick's result came up: 'Well, there you go! I thought that team was called Partick Thistle Nil.' He'd heard the three words used together so often.

I had a Great Musical Experience – I did the opera in Glasgow. Sir Alexander Gibson was conducting the orchestra. I said he was just there to catch my teeth.

I did it instead of doing the pantomime which I don't feel ready for yet . . . Some of those Scottish pantomime people are wonderful. Chick Murray has always been a hero. I'd love to work with him and Max Wall.

What I like afe the really amateur shows. The ones where midnight has to strike and you hear a wee boy going 'Ping-ping-ping-ping' with a glass twelve times. But at number nine he breaks the glass. So you hear this voice from behind the curtain going 'nine-ten-eleven-twelve.'

The Scottish press can be very hard on any kind of Scottish acts. The ones I can't stand are the ones who call you 'Bore of the Year' when they haven't even seen you perform. I made a big mistake kicking Hugh Farmer up the arse – if I'd known, I'd have poured salt on him and he'd have disappeared.

The magazines in Scotland are odd, too. The *Scottish Field* is full of pictures of big houses with moats and pheasants and weddings where all the men have those public-school haircuts, all smarmed down on the top of the head. And lots of advertisements for galoshes.

But the papers, I think, had a lot to do with the success of Scottish Nationalism . . . 'A Free Scotland' . . . That's what gave me the idea of the line: 'Free means for nothing and nothing means for free'. Frankie Miller used it in that song of his about Alcatraz, 'The Rock'.

My own MP used to be a Tory called Galbraith – rumour had it that he had once been seen in Scotland.

But I like what Dylan Thomas said about nationalism when he was asked what he thought about Welsh Nationalism: he said he had only three words to say about Welsh Nationalism and two of them were Welsh Nationalism. That's what I feel about Scottish Nationalism.

GREETINGS FROM

JIBROVI

The Great Hole

Saint Jib

Jibrovian Peasantry

— Steve Bell —

JIBROVIA

ot many people have heard of Jibrovia, let alone been there. But it's one of my favourite places for performing. It's hard to know how to describe it to the uninitiated so perhaps it's simplest just to quote from its tourist brochure:

Geography: it's actually on a peninsula although, with the heavy seas, this often becomes an island and once a fortnight, regular as clockwork, the water comes in and covers the whole place. It's a fairly sophisticated form of population control.

History: Jibrovia has never been colonised because no one who ever went there liked it much. The rest of its history is nonexistent, which makes it a very popular subject for 'O' levels.

Tourist attractions: the main attraction is the Great Hole of Jibrovia. This is where the bricks were taken from to build the Great Wall of China and there is constant wrangling with the Peking government to get them returned. Due to an oversight by the planners, the Great Hole is right in the middle of the capital, which is also called Jibrovia.

National holidays: St Jiblet's birthday is the only national holiday. St Jiblet, the patron saint of great holes, was martyred by being thrown down the Great Hole and stunned by a half-brick as he tried to get out, though in those days he was just known as plain Mr Jiblet. There is a statue to his memory in the foyer of the Edinburgh Opera House.

The national religion is the worship of manholes – there are no churches, any manhole does. Wherever a Jibrovian finds himself or herself in the world, the simple rule is just to face down a manhole for prayer.

And they have found a simple way of finding which way is down – they carry a stone taken from the rim of the Great Hole attached to a piece of string and the stone always points to down. It's known as the Jibrovian Compass. Up is 'see other end'.

The religion has few rules although young couples getting married are always taught: 'Don't be caught outside the house when the music stops'.

Language: Jibberish is the main language and it's compulsory that it's spoken in parliament like every other country.

The old Jibrovian language, which preceded Jibberish, is dying – there's only one guy knows it and nobody likes him. There is a Jibrovian language society but there are no members. Because if you learn the language, you'll have to talk to that bloke and this doesn't inspire people with any great fire to learn it.

Weather: there are never any weather reports because no one ever looks up enough to know whether it's a nice day or not. But the general rule is: when the Hole is full, it's wet; when it's empty, it's dry; when you get blown into it, either it's windy or you've had a drink.

Food: The staple diet is the jib-roll. Apart from that, jibs and jiblets are popular. Gusset soup is another traditional dish and Jibrovians keep their salt intake up by scoffing great helpings of gusset pudding. The food shortage in the seventies was solved by cannibalism – you just ate anybody you didn't like.

Transport: you can get a Jib-rover rail ricket which is extremely cheap. Unfortunately, there are no railways. But it gets you your first drink free at any Jibrovian pub.

There is little queuing necessary for buses as most of the bus stops are in the middle of ponds.

Postal services: there are no postage stamps – you just draw a wee face with a smile on it and write beside it however much you can afford.

Parcels are sent abroad by bottle. You just shove your goods in a bottle and throw it in the sea. There is a huge catapult on the top of the post office for airmail bottles. The neighbours are always complaining.

Telegrams arrive by hip flask. Postmen travel by milk float.

Dress: crocheted underwear is the national costume and is worn in the national colours. However, there is a permanent dispute about what the national colours are, which creates many problems for the national football team (see below).

Day-to-day wear for men is a tattooed three-piece suit. Fly buttons are applied with some considerable pain. The one great advantage is that it grows with you so you never need to buy a new one – although members of the Jibrovian diplomatic service suffer problems when they have to go to black-tie functions.

Entertainment and culture: the film industry is just now coming into its own in Jibrovia, although they have yet to graduate to moving picture production and films are made out of a series of slides, usually taken very fast by a man careering downhill with a stills camera. The film star's life is short as they are usually shoved over a precipice and photographed again by people taking still photos very, very quickly. This is the nearest they can get as yet to the motion picture.

Jibrovia has also developed the art of Scruff Movies, the answer to the unpleasant American Snuff Movies. Michael Foot, a national hero, has won the coveted Herbert for Best Foreign Actor in these movies for the last twelve years. He has on one occasion been pipped at the post by Patrick Moore, who has his own cult following in Jibrovia, as he is known as the only man ever to come to the country and spend much of his time looking upwards. People always fear for his safety when he visits, which accounts for him being decorated as Survivor of the Year on a number of occasions, despite the fact that there is a dreadful lack of interest in astronomy in Jibrovia.

Unfortunately, Jibrovia has been suspended for two years from the Eurovision Song Contest for crowd behaviour and dirty lyrics.

Art galleries are considered bad luck by the superstitious Jibrovians so there are very few of them and most of them are closed.

Sport and leisure: Jibrovia has never qualified for the World Cup at football and has little chance of ever so doing. The team is picked on a rota system since the game is not popular – players are drafted into it on the same basis as National Service. The only cup ever won by the team is the Greatest Mum in the World, which a neighbour of the left-winger was given by her daughter in 1978; she passed it on to the team, and it is paraded round the stadium before home games.

But Jibrovia does hope to stage the 1992 Olympics – in Glasgow, where they understand that the town planners are worshippers of great holes, too.

Sky-diving is the main national sport – it was started by St Jib, as he is now known, when he was thrown into the Great Hole.

Angling in Jibrovia consists of taking wee pieces of metal and bending them into shape.

The Jibrovian Marathon is run every spring. There is a high fatality rate since at that time of the year Jibrovia is only twenty miles long and the Marathon course is twenty-six. Thus the healthy runners fall off the edge and only the old and feeble survive. Running is also considered bad luck.

The Mr Jibrovia competition has been discontinued because no one wanted to undress and show their crocheted underwear, lest people laugh and pass remarks.

Wildlife: in the mountains there is an animal which no one has ever seen called The Lurker. It is kept in the lurker room at the zoo, but no one has ever seen it there either, since it is bad luck to look at it.

Lurker hunters go out with blindfolds on at night so as not to see the animal and you can tell if there's been a hunt if you see two blokes coming back carrying a pole with nothing hanging on it. The shrill whispers of the lurkers can be heard at night in the north of the country. Apart from man-eating whelks, lurkers are the only wild animals on Jibrovia – even the snakes there are domesticated and get taken out for walks in the park and put out at night.

Politics: the country is currently run by a coalition consisting of the Shut Your Face And Roll A Joint Party, the Have Another Biscuit Your Mother Walked Miles To Get Them Party and the We've Run Out Of Potatoes Will Chips Do Party. The loyal opposition is the Sorry Son There's No Bread You'll Have To Have Rolls Party, which ran the country until the last war.

Economy and industry: the government has recently slashed income tax by cutting out income altogether – an idea they got from Thatcher.

All Jibrovians are on a one-day week to keep in line with the clergy. This is the result of a hard-fought campaign for Parity With Rome.

Main exports are gussets, waterbeds and oil. A minor export is that of stanchions for the goalposts of second-division clubs everywhere. Jibrovian waterbeds are of simple construction – they consist entirely of the sea. A kingsize bed is the ocean and a storm is an orgy on a Jibrovian waterbed.

A Jibrovian oil rig is a big jar of Brylcreem on legs. There are

1. The Customs post in Jibrovia. Few greyhounds get past without a strip search.

Below: Jibrovian quantity surveyor looking for the way down.

2. Canute-worship is still popular in Jibrovia. So is feeding ducks.

3. Jibrovian at prayer.

4. The editor of Jibrovia's Taylor and Cutter showing off.

frequently Brylcreem slicks which the legendary Jibrovian fire-fighter, Green McNair, is called on to battle with. This he does using a stoutly rolled-up newspaper. (No one else will join the fire brigade in Jibrovia because it often involves looking up in the air. Hence tourists are advised to book ground-floor rooms wherever possible.)

Defence: the entire defence budget is spent on squibs.

A long-running war with Switzerland, whom Jibrovia challenged to a Best of Three in the forties, continues to be waged by the navies of both countries. There are still children in Jibrovia waiting for their fathers to come back from the planned invasion of Switzerland in 1948. It would appear that the navy invasion force is prospering as messages come back from the front in very expensive bottles, sometimes with liquor still in them.

There is also a Jibrovian Home Guard, whose hero of legend is King Canute. They train by sitting in folding chairs round ponds telling the water to go back. If the water remains where it is, they then feed the ducks from large plastic bags with large plastic pieces of bread and when the bread is finished try to make the ducks go back.

Service in this branch of the Home Guard is voluntary which means that hardly anybody does it unless the weather is just right. The ducks have also been getting restless in recent years and are not as co-operative as they once were.

Education: the teacher shortage has been completely solved in Jibrovia – all the schools have been closed. The problem of the lack of teaching staff had been getting everyone down for a number of years so the government felt this was the simplest solution.

There is, however, a very active Cub movement, based on Baden Powell's model except for the fact that the Cubs say: 'Jib, Jib, Jib' at the start of meetings.

Passport procedures and embassy facilities: no visas are necessary and if you lose your passport you can be issued with a Jibrovian one which is just a school jotter with a drawing of your face inside it.

The British Ambassador is a photograph. (This was introduced as a recent economy measure.)

National Anthem: 'Ohhhh, Jibrovia'.

> 'Forward Jibrovia,
> With gussets to the fore!' (Repeat.)

(This should be sung as though a Christmas tree is being pulled slowly out of your anus. Thus: 'Ohhhhhhaaaaaahhhhh Jib-rooooooovia, Fooooorward, Jibroooooovia' etc.)

The Jibrovian World Cup Song, like the stadium, has not been completed yet but starts off thus:

> 'Viva Jibrovia
> From the Great Hole to the Sea.'

National Motto: Je Ne Sais Quoi.
(Translated this means: 'Fuck the begrudgers'.)

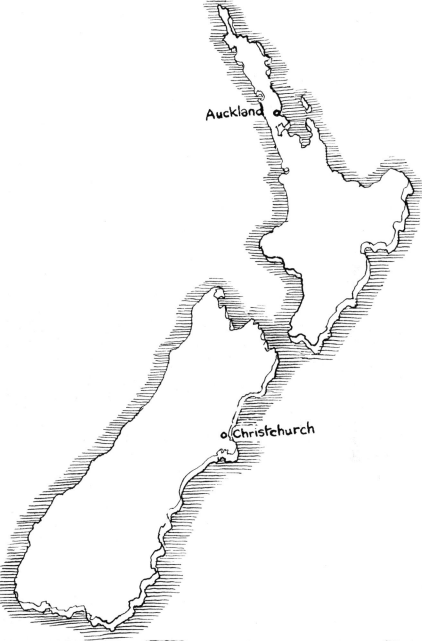

Auckland

Christchurch

NEW ZEALAND

ew Zealand is another place where the politics have absolutely no relation to the people there. The people are great. Their prime minister's a half-wit.

There's also been a lot of gerrymandering of the constituencies in the past. The farmlands get all the seats and the socialists are the wee dots in the middle of the dart board that get fucked over all the time.

We came across some great Maoris there – a rock and roll band that we found playing on top of a mountain for some reason. A big Maori bloke who sings country wanted to do one of my songs so he gave me an earring for it, with a clock in it. I don't think it was for any big record deal or anything – I think he did it like they do in the Highlands in Scotland: you make your own records and take them and flog them round the lounge bars.

In Hamilton it was very strange. It was this big sea of tartan greeted you as you came on stage – every Scot in town.

And in Dunedin it rained on stage. In fact, the act that performed there before me – an opera singer – did the whole show in a fur coat because the weather was so inclement. It must be the only place in the world where the audience is covered and the performer is in the open.

It was very disturbing – there was a puddle getting nearer and nearer my instruments and it was almost too cold to play so a guy threw me up his jacket.

Still, it wasn't too hard to appeal to local humour – the Prime Minister's a walking joke after all: 'Piggy' Muldoon, what a name.

* HAVE YOU HUGGED *
YOUR HORSE TODAY ?
JUSTIN DISCOUNT BOOTS AND COWBOY OUTFITTERS · JUSTIN, TEX

Meet Me At
HOLIDAY ROLLER RINK
2920 Carson   Ft. Worth   Haltom City, Tex
838-5738

A Law We Can
LIVE WITH 55

HQG·516

Above: No, to the first question. No, to the
question on the left. And Come off it, to the
statement on the right.

Left: Sharing a joke with The Invisible Man
in Toronto.

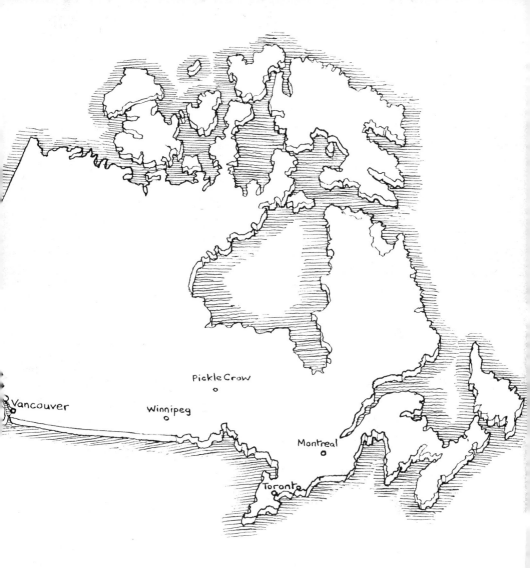

Pickle Crow

Vancouver

Winnipeg

Montreal

Toronto

CANADA

A guy walking along the street in Glasgow. He's just back from Canada where he's emigrated and he thinks he's made it. They're amazing these blokes – I met one in Barbados who asked me how a Scot could afford to go to Barbados – *pissoff* – anyway this bloke is walking along the street trying to look rich in his suit. He sees a wee boy, aged about nine, having a smoke – Capstan full strength.

'That's a damn disgrace. A little boy like you having a cigarette at your age.'

'Aw – that's nothin'. Last night I was makin' love tae a lassie of nine.'

'That is *appalling*! What was her name?'

'Cannae remember – I was pissed.'

One time I was in Toronto when Yul Brynner was performing in *Odysseus*. And I happened to know the woman who was doing the promotion stuff for it. Before he went on she told him there would be a bloke in the front row who looked like Jesus Christ. So he came on stage and delivered all of his opening lines straight at me. I didn't know where to look.

In Canada, the Irish jokes are Newfoundland jokes. And as soon as I heard them being told I knew instinctively that I was going to like Newfies. And in Denmark, the Finns were the brunt of all the jokes. So I said what is it that you don't like about the Finns? 'Aw, they're drunk all the time.' So I thought I bet I like every Finn I meet and that was true as well. Though I think they stopped telling the Polish jokes very rapidly in America which just shows you the hypocrisy of it all. These comics making a living out of jokes that say the Poles are dirty and unhygienic and stupid and then they appear on telly saying how wonderful the Polish people are.

You have to get used to the overpowering smell of aftershave and perfume when performing in North America. They overdo it a bit on that front. A lot of people seem to be in constant terror of smelling like a human being so they shower all the time and put deodorants on. In a concert hall you get all the smells mixed together and it hits you like a brick wall, a sugary pink wall that makes your eyes burn. When you play to the younger ones, the rock venues, the brick wall smells of dope. I'd never experienced that level of dope in the air, it's quite stunning. The air is blue with marijuana. You get quite a buzz from it even without smoking, very loose, very pleasant.

In Hamilton, Ontario, I hold the record for the bar takings at a concert in the place there. The last time I was there the promoter, John McQuaig, had a bet on with Jimmy the manager that we would break the bar record again and it was broken by the time I arrived. I'm not sure whether to be proud of that or not.

Canada's an odd country to tour. It's like New Zealand. There's nobody there. Dense population and then wilderness.

We were in the French quarter in Montreal which was a real treat, although I don't speak French beyond being able to book a room for the night. However, I learned a lesson when I was with the Humble-bums in Belgium because I had gone up to a guy to buy something and said 'D'you speak English?' And he said: 'not today'. It was a real lesson to me that you should say 'Excuse me, I'm sorry I don't speak your language, do you speak English?' Because the only French I got at school was how to order a drink in Morocco and if the barman then bursts into conversation about the leaves falling off the trees, I'm knackered.

Ice hockey fascinates me. I used to support the Boston Bruins. And the players – instead of putting their money in pubs like football players in Britain do when they're getting ready to retire – buy a wee lake . . . 'Aye, I think I'll have one of these, please.' And they put Finnish log cabins around them. And they rent them out to people who want to be in the wilderness – you hop on a flying-boat, land on the lake and get dropped off. It's an alarming experience I should imagine – the pilots all wear diver's watches, which for some reason ordinary pilots seem to wear, too. I had a diver's watch once – had to kill a diver to get it . . But why should an ordinary pilot have to wear a diver's watch? It doesn't exactly inspire great confidence. So that's how they make their money – punters going off for ten days in the wilds with bears and trout and lions and salmon.

I met a gangster fellow in Boston and he took a liking to me and he took me to see the Bruins. I was telling another guy that night that

I'd just seen them and he was so angry because he'd been on the waiting list for three months and I had just swanned in.

I wouldn't like to be a gangster in Canada. You'd never know when you were out having a nice time in the wilderness if the bloke riding by on horseback was a plain clothes Mountie or a punter having a canter.

But I don't think I'll ever get used to all that open space out there. Where I grew up, the rooms were so small you could turn the light out and be in bed before it was dark.

HEAVEN AND HELL

SteveBell

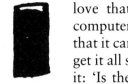love that Isaac Asimov story about the ultimate computer – they have absolutely everything in it so that it can answer anything. And so they get it ready, get it all set up, have all the systems working and ask it: 'Is there a God?' And suddenly all the working parts stop and the answer comes up: 'There Is Now.'

When I was working in Biafra there was a bloke there from Northumbria and his father had died and had left him a message to go and look for an old tin in the garage. So he did and found inside a load of money and instructions to go down to the local and blow the lot and not come back with any change. Which I think is a nice way to deal with it all.

I can't understand the reverence with which the whole business is still treated. It's about ten years since I did the crucifixion and yet it's listed under Religious Affairs at Radio Clyde.

I like what Lenny Bruce said about Jesus – that if he'd been alive in the twentieth century people would be wandering around with a wee electric chair hanging round their necks.

But if Jesus was a Jew – how come he's got a Mexican first name?

Someone said that if they had a *Which?* report on religions, the Jewish faith would come off worst because of all the things you can't do and don't get but I think the Wee Frees must run them pretty close.

But you know when everything's broken down and it's all particles and solar systems you start to wonder if you're just part of a chair leg or a teacup or something . . . So if you see me wearing a golden teacup round my neck on every seventh Sunday shouting 'Follow me', you'll know I was right. If not, you'll know there must have been something in my tea.

My cousin, who's a priest, was due to go off and work in Brazil and I think he was really looking forward to the idea but at the last moment he was sent to Bangladesh instead. So I told my dad that he'd been hoping for cha-cha-cha and what he was getting was neewowowwooo; and it's the first time I think I've got my dad to laugh at a religious joke because he's a good Catholic.

Elvis Presley and Steve McQueen are in heaven and they decide that they'll have a party. So Elvis and Steve McQueen agree to arrange the booze. And they send Isabel Barnett out for the tea-cakes.

The Brontë's brother wanted to make the point that you could die standing up. So just as he was about to cop it he got out of bed and staggered to the mantlepiece and leant against it and died standing up. Proved his point.

What I'd like to have on my tombstone is just 'the Big Yin' . . . though I like the one that a waiter in Paris is supposed to have: 'God finally caught his attention'.

I never know why people bother about my soul when I tell blasphemous jokes – after all, it's me that goes to hell. That's where you get sent if you tell jokes like: 'What's blue and fucks old ladies? – Hypothermia.'

Miles Davis dies and goes down to hell. He feels a bit depressed about it naturally enough. Then he bumps into Hoagy Carmichael who says: 'Hi – fancy coming along for a jam tonight?' So he thinks – this can't be that bad. Then he's off to his room and in the corridor he meets Bix Beiderbecke who says that he's playing in the jam too and he's got a new trumpet for him – which turns out to be perfect, just what he wanted. So the time for the jam session comes and he goes into the room where they're all playing and there are all the greatest jazz musicians there – a real all-star band, all with their instruments. He can't believe it. It's fantastic. Then Duke Ellington calls them all to order. And the band starts playing 'Viva Espana'.

My idea of hell is those parties you get invited to after shows where you arrive at the house and everyone's sitting there in a semi-circle waiting for you to perform. Either that or spending years and years in prison and no one to give a cuddle to. Though sometimes just before I'm about to go on and there's no way out you wish you could just disappear . . . comics are so neurotic, but I don't go for all that 'comedy is a very serious business' which you hear some comedians saying – though quite often when they do it, it is.

Still you can't worry too much about the future. Life is not a rehearsal.

When they were planning the Pope's visit to Glasgow they had to dig up lots of trees in Bellahouston Park so that more punters could get a look at him. And there was an enormous fuss about it with all the Orange mob saying: 'Aye, they're taking away trees today – they'll be taking away Protestants tomorrow.'

The business of trying to get the Catholic and Protestant bits of the church together seems a bit daft – unless of course they see the Church as being in the same sort of trouble as football and they think they should get involved in a bit of ground-sharing, split the cost of the floodlights sort of thing. In a way it's the same sort of problem: these great big buildings that are used only once a week or once a fortnight and teams that used to draw millions of fans every week and now they're playing to two men and a dog and an empty packet of crisps. So I suppose it makes sense to amalgamate and hope that you can fill the grounds and pay the bills that way. But where does it leave the Queen, if the Pope is to be the Number One? She'll not settle for the assistant-manager's job, I would imagine . . .

I feel sorry for that woman who wants to become a priest and she keeps popping up and talking about it – because presumably now that they're talking about a merger, her chances are forever scuppered. Though if they *don't* allow the Church of England ministers to stay married, if they insist that they become celibate like the Roman Catholic priests, it's going to raise an extremely interesting ecumenical dilemma: who's going to cut the flowers and make the sandwiches at the bazaar? That's what the Archbishop of Canterbury should be considering. Years of tradition that has been fought for and people have been martyred for can't be thrown away, is what I imagine a good Protestant would think. Who's going to be Akela to the Cubs if vicars don't have wives?

Still, who'd be a vicar? The number of times people must ask you if you'd like more tea.

It's strange remembering going to communion in Partick on a Sunday morning. You had to fast from midnight and I'll never forget that empty feeling as you went to church without your breakfast – all for God. I wrote a poem about it:

Fasted from midnight
And slowed from emptiness
Walking without laughter
In case my guardian angel should hear
And tell God.
Keeping my eyes hooded during consecration
In case I should catch a glimpse of God
And go blind.
Fighting the urge to peel my communion
From the roof of my mouth
With my index finger,
Letting my mouth's ceiling
Become the lips of my soul.

It's a funny feeling now that you don't believe any more when you look back on yourself as a person that did believe. Because it was dead cosy, I must admit. Everything fell into place in those days . . . the comforting things around you – like your favourite pencil and ruler – which would have a special taste to it and you would write your name in big letters on one side and your address – always ending in The World, The Universe – on the other side. Enough of that.

Some people are anti-Catholic without knowing why. I came across a guy, a skinhead, in Chelsea and he had 'South London Skins' written on his cheek. He had other tattoos on his forehead and a tattooed spider crawling up his jaw. And he had one on the side of his neck all blotted out, they do it with a laser I think. So I asked him: 'What was that one?' 'The Red Hand of Ulster'. 'Why d'you get it scrubbed out?' 'Big Irishmen in pubs were always going to take my head off.' He was a Londoner and wasn't the slightest bit interested in the Orange Order and probably wouldn't have known King Billy from a crack in the pavement, but it was a rebellion thing. Not the brightest place in the world to put something like that – on your neck. But I suppose it was very handy for any Republican he bumped into a pub – Tear Here. I was wondering how he was going to feel when he was fifty, with 'South London Skins' tattooed on his face. There was no way he could take it off without looking horrendous; and he was about eighteen. His girlfriend had 'Belsen Was a Gas' tattooed on her arm. Takes a lot of bottle – though in their case I think it took a lot of thickness. Unless he can con some plastic surgeon to whip them all off for him . . .

Nearly Forty

Jesus Christ, I'm nearly forty
My pubic hair is turning grey.
I can't cut the mustard like I used to.
They say it's downhill all the way.

Please don't put me by the seaside.
Don't shout as though my ears don't work.
Never let me pee my trousers.
Don't let me dribble down my shirt.

Amen.

THOUGHTS
THAT
SUSTAIN ME

Never trust a man who, when he's alone in a room with a tea-cosy, doesn't try it on.

The more you know the less the better.

You can take a horse to water but if you ever do just remember how a wet horse smells.

If all Agatha Christie's books were laid end to end, it'd still be raining in Glasgow.

Don't go down the mine, Daddy, there's plenty of slack in your trousers.

When the vulture flies sideways, the moon has hair on his upper lip. (Old Arabic saying that loses something in translation.)

I'm a warbaby. I cry easily.

A bird in the hand invariably shits on your wrist.

My karma ran over my dogma.

A well-balanced person has a drink in each hand.

You're not drunk if you can lie on the floor without holding on.

When things are tough, remember the Dunkirk Spirit – run like hell.

If I got married again, I'd be a bigyinamist.

Life is like a Japanese fish – you have to cut a slice and eat it raw.

And some cheery insults:

Champagne bubbles get up your nose and you get up mine.

Leave me alone – I don't come to your work and tell you how to sweep up.

If I had a voice like yours, I'd teach my arse to sing.

What do you do for a face when King Kong wants his arse back?

(To big-mouthed people): a pal of mine lived in the country. He had this beautiful horse. And one time it got very sick. So the vet came to look at it. And he shook his head . . . 'No, I'm afraid there's nothing I can do. What it needs if the kiss of life and there's no one can give it.' I wish you'd been there – that horse would be alive today.

You suffer from cerebral dysentery – a rush of shit to the head.

You've obviously never had haemorrhoids in your life – you're a perfect arsehole.

Someone should take your mouth away and fit it with a drawbridge.

And a ditty that calls to mind the glens when we are far from home

I woke up with an aching head
As usual.
I can't remember going to bed
As usual.
My stomach's feeling very queer,
There's a thunderstorm in my right ear,
It must have been McEwan's beer
As usual.

We sucked the drinks up like a hoover
As usual.
The cheap wine and the paint remover
As usual.
And somewhere deep inside my brain,
I seem to hear a diesel train,
And I promise not to drink again
As usual.

I woke up in a public park
As usual.
I must have crawled there after dark
As usual.
I'd better see how much I've got,
Oh, Jesus Christ, I've spent the lot,
I must have been a drunken sot
As usual.

If you've enjoyed reading this book half as much as I've enjoyed putting it together, then I'll have enjoyed putting it together twice as much as you've enjoyed reading it.

184